T0326996

"There are few pleasures as dis_____
then chasing it with a spirited c_____
is loaded with that lovely feeli_____
set of films; Norris and Higgins make excellent tour guides
who can lead us into the vast landscape of world cinema."

—**Josh Jeter**, producer of Terrence Malick's
A Hidden Life

"Norris and Higgins seem to engage movies for the same
reason I do: in the faith that better is possible and that good
stories show us the way. Their experience of said stories and
which stories have the most meaning for them are, of course,
different from my own. *But isn't that the gift?* In the movies
they have invited us to, I get to experience the world through
their eyes, and my own experience is broadened. *What will we
choose to do with the broadening of our experiences?* This
is the charge these two movie lovers so deftly set before us."

—**Melvin Bray**, equity designer and author of
Better: Waking Up to Who We Could Be

"As a fan of Kathleen Norris's *Cloister Walk* and *Dakota*, I
loved reading her honest engagement with various films in
this book. Higgins and Norris add to a conversation that
the filmmaker has begun and draw from their experience of
life to give these humble films more depth. I wish there was
more writing about films like it. I feel my perspective about
the world widening through it."

—**Lee Isaac Chung**, director of *Minari* and *Twisters*

"In *A Whole Life in Twelve Movies*, Norris and Higgins do
what they do so well: weave together stories and commentary that remind us what it means to be human, to long for
love and connection, and to search the world around us for

moments of kinship as we carry grief, joy, healing, and longing inside our own hearts. Art is powerful, and in the pages of this book you'll find an incredible guide into one of the most effective forms of art—film—to explore our connection to ourselves, spirituality, and one another. Whether you're an avid movie watcher or hoping to dive into these films for the first time, please read this book and let it lead you into curiosity and wonder. You'll be so glad you did."

—**Kaitlin B. Curtice**, award-winning author of
Native, *Living Resistance*, and *Winter's Gifts*

"This book is a loving embrace of a new way of seeing—which used to be an old way of seeing. With eyes and souls wide open, Norris and Higgins dare to engage cinema on its deepest and most meaningful levels; they dare to believe in it as art. Most scandalously of all, they dare to believe movies can teach us how to live better, if only we'd allow them to. This book is a treasure."

—**Scott Teems**, writer-director, *Rectify*,
Narcos: Mexico, and *The Quarry*

A WHOLE LIFE IN
TWELVE MOVIES

PREVIOUS BOOKS BY AUTHORS

Kathleen Norris

Acedia and Me: A Marriage, Monks, and a Writer's Life

The Quotidian Mysteries: Laundry, Liturgy, and "Women's Work"

The Virgin of Bennington

Amazing Grace: A Vocabulary of Faith

The Cloister Walk

Dakota: A Spiritual Biography

Journey: New and Selected Poems

Little Girls in Church

Gareth Higgins

How Not to Be Afraid: Seven Ways to Live When Everything Seems Terrifying

How Movies Helped Save My Soul

Cinematic States: Stories We Tell, the American Dreamlife, and How to Understand Everything

The Seventh Story: Us, Them, and the End of Violence (with Brian McLaren)

Cory and the Seventh Story (with Brian McLaren)

A WHOLE LIFE IN TWELVE MOVIES

A CINEMATIC JOURNEY TO A DEEPER SPIRITUALITY

KATHLEEN NORRIS
AND GARETH HIGGINS

Brazos Press
a division of Baker Publishing Group
BrazosPress.com

Published by Brazos Press
a division of Baker Publishing Group
Grand Rapids, Michigan
BrazosPress.com

Printed in the United States of America

Library of Congress Cataloging-in-Publication Data
Names: Norris, Kathleen, 1947– author. | Higgins, Gareth I., author.
Title: A whole life in twelve movies : a cinematic journey to a deeper spirituality / Kathleen Norris and Gareth Higgins.
Description: Grand Rapids : Brazos Press, a division of Baker Publishing Group, 2024. | Includes bibliographical references.
Identifiers: LCCN 2024013558 | ISBN 9781587436338 (paperback) | ISBN 9781587436543 (casebound) | ISBN 9781493447947 (ebook)
Subjects: LCSH: Motion pictures—Reviews. | Spirituality. | Conduct of life.
Classification: LCC PN1995 .N67 2024 | DDC 791.43/75—dc23/eng/20240402
LC record available at https://lccn.loc.gov/2024013558

Earlier versions of brief parts of the text have been previously published: portions of Gareth's essays on *Paterson* ("A Poetic Vision," *Sojourners*, March 2017, https://sojo.net/magazine/march-2017/poetic-vision) and *Babette's Feast* (Fuller Seminary/Reel Spirituality), and Kathleen's essay on *Paterson* ("Odd Jobs," October 11, 2020, Soul Telegram).

Cover design by Laura Powell

Published in association with The Bindery Agency, www.TheBinderyAgency.com.

24 25 26 27 28 29 30   7 6 5 4 3 2 1

For the new generation:
Gabriella, Maria, Eve, Sabrina
—KN

For Mike Riddell,
who helped me love life as
much as I love movies
—GH

It has been said that we dream our lives, and if we do not awaken to this, they can be over before we know it.

Cinema is perhaps our most dreamlike art form, and if we learn to dream with it and reflect on those dreams, we may well experience richer, deeper, and more creative, connected, and even courageous lives. We're inviting you to reflect together on the journey of a whole human life, from birth to death, through the dreamworld of the movies. We'll reflect on twelve films, look at ourselves, stretch our horizons into the future, and reimagine the past.

Let's begin.

CONTENTS

Contents

FOREWORD

James Martin, SJ

Reading this beautiful book is like having an endlessly fascinating conversation with two friends about film, when those two friends are always wise, thoughtful, and funny and have inspiring things to say about the movies they love. They invite the reader to consider films that have something to tell us about how best to live: how we can protect the innocence of children, how we can find a job that pays the bills and also nourish a vocation in the arts, how we can counter greed and violence with self-sacrificing love, and how we might choose to remember our lives once they've ended. Movies for every stage of life.

I was especially taken by their conversation about one of my all-time favorite films, *Babette's Feast*, a gem of a movie about a mysterious visitor to a small nineteenth-century Danish community, which always stirs good conversation. I know few people who are unmoved by this gorgeous movie, based on a short story by Isak Dinesen, author of

Out of Africa. Gareth comes at the film one way—seeing it as a story about priorities; Kathleen comes at it another, seeing it as a kind of parable. It's a testimony to their love of that film—and all films under consideration—that no matter which perspective appeals to you, the other one will have you nodding your head and saying, "I never thought about it like that!"

Of course, the best way to approach this book would be to watch these films with a friend, discuss them afterward, then turn to Gareth and Kathleen. Or, if you're more of a loner, you might watch them privately and then have a kind of virtual conversation with these two authors. For me, the first thing I want to do after watching a powerful film is see what others have to say about it. At heart, it's a desire for conversation, for learning, and for being challenged. This book is an answer to those common desires.

Some of the films in this book are well known, others are not. None of them are specifically religious, but they insist that human beings are much more than flesh and blood. Coming from directors and screenwriters of diverse backgrounds, they reveal that common to us all is a desire to live more fully and to draw on kindness, mercy, generosity, and love to help us live more humanely in this world. In keeping with this book's spirit of hospitality, the authors provide a list of suggested questions at the end of each chapter to help the reader engage with the film and to keep the conversation going.

Enjoy the conversation you are about to have!

INTRODUCTION

Kathleen Norris: "It's a Beautiful Day"

Until I watched *The Wizard of Oz*, I had little idea of the power of films. I'd seen only movies shot in black and white and gasped when Dorothy opened the door of her Kansas farmhouse and entered a world saturated with color. I spent childhood summers in western South Dakota and often saw rainbows appear after violent storms. I had never considered that there was a world up there populated by witches, a wizard, and a host of other fascinating creatures.

The flying monkeys ordered by an evil witch to seize Dorothy and her companions scared me. But the witch's hourglass frightened me more as its sand flowed steadily to the bottom, indicating that Dorothy and her friends had little time left to live. My belief that all movies had happy endings was diminishing with that sand.

It was not lost on me that Dorothy saves herself by following her instinct to help a friend in need. And the witch's lament, that "a good little girl like you could destroy my beautiful wickedness," introduced me to a vast literary and

1

cinematic heritage in which everything from the Bible to *The Lord of the Rings* and *Harry Potter* insists that while evil can do significant damage, the good will find a way to overcome it. When as an adult I encountered the ancient Christian notion of "the gift of tears," considered a divine gift because tears awaken our compassion, I remembered that witch and was comforted by the thought that even my worst inclinations could be melted and redeemed.

When Dorothy wakes after the tornado has passed and finds herself at home, in her own bed, she is startled to see that her friends from Oz are people she's known all along, farmhands and a traveling magician/con artist. That's a lesson for all of us, to better value the people we encounter every day and often take for granted. Maybe the best way to watch *The Wizard of Oz*, and all other good films, is as a child would see them, allowing a good story to lead you into unimagined worlds.

▲▼▲

We yearn for the illumination that helps us make life worth living and leave our world better than we found it. In times when it seems too dark to see, we welcome light from any quarter. This book is in part a celebration of a friendship that came as a flash of light when Gareth Higgins and I met at a conference on art and spirituality and quickly realized that we needed to collaborate on writing about films.

Our working title for this book was "It's a Beautiful Day," a line from the Coen brothers' darkly comic masterpiece *Fargo*. After audiences have witnessed a violent kidnapping and a host of murders, it can feel jarring to hear our heroine, the indomitable (and pregnant) police officer Marge, say, "It's a beautiful day." But it's the essence of the film. *Fargo* is a morality tale that rejects nihilism and offers a perfect illustration of St. Paul's warning that "the wages of sin is death" (Rom. 6:23).

The film features people tempted by greed and the desire for power as they sink deeper into crime, violence, and bad ends. Marge has just seen the man in the back seat murder his accomplice in a brutal way, and his sly, dead-eye expression indicates that he'd kill her if he had the chance. But she's not afraid of him. As the moral center of the film, she is relentless. After naming the other people she knows he's killed, she asks, "And for what? A little bit of money? There's more to life than a little money, you know; don't you know that?" We realize that the man will never realize that, and as we hear the sirens of backup police officers and an ambulance approaching, Marge sighs and says, "Well, I just don't understand it." And we hope she never will.

Fargo, like many films discussed in this book, does not provide easy entertainment. Our intent is that they will invite all of us to a deeper understanding of human nature and spirituality and will inform our desire to live better and more fulfilled lives. As you read this book, we hope the observation that "it's a beautiful day" will remain with you, an affirmation of the human ability to find redemption in all situations and circumstances.

Gareth Higgins: Thinking about Cinema and Spirituality

> You gotta say something with a movie. Otherwise, what's the point of making it?
>
> —Martin Scorsese

Cinema is nothing if not light. In its most life-giving forms, it illuminates not only the characters, images, and stories on screen but also those of us who are watching. In this book, we reflect cinematic light on the life cycle of a human being, from before birth to after death. While each chapter focuses primarily on one film, others are mentioned along the way, and we recommend further viewing at the end of the book to go deeper with the themes.

One way to use this book is to read one chapter and watch one movie each month over the course of a year—of course, you can do it much quicker than that if you prefer. However long you take, bear in mind that there are two chapters (3 and 7) where we have chosen two films. To stay with the spirit of the "twelve movies" announced in the title of this book, you could watch just one per chapter, but we think the films in those chapters are companion pieces that fit very well together and even help interpret each other.

The book is rooted in the idea that a great film is what results when humane wisdom and grace—and technical and aesthetic craft operating at their highest frequencies—*kiss each other*, and that great cinema is for everyone.

Whether you are a seasoned movie lover or a dabbler, a long-term contemplative or an entry-level mystic, we hope that you will find something meaningful here for your life's journey. We are inviting you to a kind of liturgy for experiencing images, sounds, words, and stories in a sacramental way. This takes conscious intent and a bit of ritual, and with that in mind, we're offering some principles that can help you go deeper into movies.

There are three ways to read this book. You can watch the movie before reading our essays, read the essays before watching the movie, or just read the essays and not watch the movie at all. Viewing options change regularly, but if you can't find a movie on a streaming service or at your local library, DVDs and Blu-rays are widely available online.

Movies are best experienced without too much analysis, but keep in mind that a film is not only about what it's about but *how* it's about what it's about. A story may matter less than image, sound, and the invitation to let the film change you. That said, for narrative films with "something to say," consider the following questions as you watch.

Perspective
Whose point of view is being presented: who gets to speak, and who doesn't?

Context and Consequences
How are motivations, actions, and consequences depicted? The portrayal of violence, close relationships, and societal change are three good examples of where this question can be useful. Does the movie move us to value life or to diminish it?

Learning
What did you not know before seeing this movie?

Inspiration
What do you want more of or less of after watching it?

Seeing
Cinema should be approached differently than literature or music. See movies with the best screen and sound and let your eyes wander. Who or what dominates the frame? Who is looking at whom? What colors and contrasts emerge? How does the light dance? What do you see?

Embodiment
Reflect on how a movie can embody its theme—*Paterson* (about a poet, discussed in chapter 5) has the rhythm of a

poem; *Requiem for a Dream* (about desperation) feels like a nightmare; *Into Great Silence* (about a monastery, discussed in chapter 12) is like a meditation.

Origin

Knowing something about where the movie comes from can enhance or confuse. For instance, Godfrey Reggio has often said that he isn't sure what his masterpiece, *Koyaanisqatsi*, is about, and Paul Schrader takes a more pessimistic view of his *First Reformed* than I do; but knowing that Juliette Binoche and Benoît Magimel were lovers before they were costars in *The Pot-au-Feu* deepened my engagement with that film's sketch of love and loss. And Kathleen says that knowing director Hirokazu Kore-eda included both non-actors and professionals in *After Life* enhanced her enjoyment of the film.

"Facts"

A movie does not have to be "realistic" to be truthful.

You

Different people will respond in different ways to the same movie because no one carries the same story and perspective. There is no one correct response to a film. Just bring your open heart and curious mind, respecting how the movie began as someone else's dream. Let it connect with your memories, hopes, pain, and possibilities.

▲▼▲

And remember: Sometimes a movie is just a movie. It doesn't have to have a "story" to be transcendent, and trying to make sense of it all can dilute the experience of watching.

A movie is sometimes best enjoyed by allowing it to unfold, mingle with our subconscious, and take us out into the world of wonder and shadow with something new.

It's worth noting that this book is, of course, not about everything that happens in a life but rather some of the stages and themes that usually occur as we age. It's also not a comprehensive overview of cinema. We omit many films and themes that could easily be included, but we hope that our selection is a meaningful starting point. We are inviting you into a conversation about how to *be* and how to *become*. As the Indian American director Mira Nair says, it is vital that we try to "transcend our boundaries with the other"—to imagine the world through the eyes of people who have different experiences of life.[1] Seeing ourselves mirrored by others enables us to grow and to feel less alone. With that in mind, we have consciously attempted to offer a range of movies from different parts of the world and perspectives.

Filmmaking is a collaborative art that emerged with the assumption that watching would be a shared experience. Even though how we watch movies has changed, there's something inherently communal in engaging a film that has been viewed by people around the world. Kathleen and I are both spiritual seekers, and we assume that if you're reading this, you're one too. And while she and I each come from a religious tradition, this book is intended for anyone open to how cinema can illuminate the spiritual path.

As *spirituality* is such a vague and ill-defined term, we want to make a brief statement about how we understand the word. One favorite definition comes from the Jesuit theologian Stephen Sundborg: "lived relationship with mystery,"[2] to which we'd add, *leading us to grow in the experience of union with love.* A love worthy of the name is not at all

7

vague but consists of concrete actions taken for the sake of the good. We believe that the films we've chosen reflect spirituality in this sense, answering our basic need for art that's steeped in the mystery of life, offering hope without denying real human suffering.

The chapters here imagine the arc of a life's journey, from waiting to be born until after death, allowing us to explore how cinematic artists have pondered the meaning of existence. By including questions at the end of each chapter we hope to engage you in a conversation about how to take life seriously without taking ourselves too seriously. There's no obligation to respond to all the questions; just choose the ones you consider most life-giving. But we suggest that with every movie you begin with the same three questions:

What do you remember most about the movie—what stands out for you?

What was a highlight for you, and a lowlight?

What questions does the film raise for your own life or for the world as you see it?

A Place to Begin

To get started, we recommend two short films. *The Dam Keeper* (USA, 2014, directed by Robert Kondo and Daisuke Tsutsumi, cowritten with John Henry Hinkel) and *The Red Balloon* (France, 1956, directed and written by Albert Lamorisse) are eighteen and thirty-four minutes long, respectively, but contain centuries of wisdom about life, innocence, suffering, and healing. Take a look at them, and afterward consider the principles above. See where they take you.

1

WAITING TO BE BORN

2001: A Space Odyssey (UK/USA, 1968)

Directed by Stanley Kubrick, written by Stanley Kubrick and Arthur C. Clarke

Prehistoric apes unveil violence as survival instinct, and technology dances with the paradox of killing (which closes off possibility) and discovery (which embodies it). Tracing the evolution of humanity through self-awareness and selfishness to a future stage of cosmic beneficence, *2001: A Space Odyssey* hinges on one person's response to the suffering of another.

2001 was a great cinematic leap forward; no one had seen anything like this before its release in 1968. Its themes are wide: humans' relationship with technology, how relating through computer screens has changed us for the worse and the better, the journey toward emotional maturity, and the ultimate questions of our existence.

Gareth

Take a moment to reflect on how we got here—the sheer improbability of it, the physical endurance of the one who birthed you, the hope embodied by the simple fact of your arrival. I haven't had the easiest life, and neither have you—yet such reflection on my birth leaves me shaking my head in awe. Beyond that, taking birth seriously helps heal the fear of death.

If you wanted to illustrate what it is to gestate, what it is to wait, and what it is to be born, you might show *2001: A Space Odyssey*. Among other things, and despite having no lead female character, it's a metaphor for pregnancy. I have no idea what being pregnant is like, of course, but I was once in a womb for nine months (eight and a half, to be exact; apparently I couldn't wait to be born). Even without conscious memories of that, I feel that understanding more about the first thing that happened to us might help us understand more of what has happened since and what's happening now.

A friend used to say that if a baby in utero somehow learned what birth would be like—leaving comfort to descend a suffocating tunnel to be greeted by blinding lights and huge strangers—the baby might choose to stay put. It is a struggle to be born, and that harrowing journey might appear to a newly delivered baby to be the end of life. Birth is a kind of death. Each of us deserves more credit than we may allow ourselves for just getting here. But before the getting here there is the not knowing, and the best response to that is contemplation.

▲▼▲

Active contemplation finds the depths of the universe both outside *and* inside us, making us smaller and larger at the same time. Kubrick's *2001* is a cinematic contemplative liturgy. Even its beginning has a beginning before that, an annunciatory overture featuring apes and bones, alluding to where we've come from. We see violence and mutual suspicion as a way of life—that from which we must turn. Exploration—that to which we are invited. Love between family members and friends—that which roots us. More exploration. Bad computer. More violence as a way of life. Very bad computer. Shut down. More exploration. Invitation. Journey. Shattered glass. Rebirth. Everything.

Perhaps *liturgy* isn't the best word. In *2001* we discover a format not only for a "religious" experience but for the experience of *life*. It's a film that can help us value the lives we are living—cosmic selves, stardust, golden. And at the everyday level, it's a mirror to the experience of waiting that constitutes so much of life.

When astronaut David Bowman (the name evokes both a primal hunter and the biblical character known as "friend of God") allows himself to be transported into our future, it's because he has *waited*. The reason the movie takes so long is because *life does*. This is *waiting* both in the sense of allowing time to do what time does and also in the sense of waiting on others, waiting as service. Risking his life to rescue a colleague, and the tenderness of how he picks him up even with mechanical arms, may ultimately fail to save his friend, but it signals to the Being(s) running the show that he is worthy. That he would go that far to rescue someone is one way to prove that he is truly human.

After this sacrifice, David is sent through a Star Gate (not unlike a birth canal) to *become* what's next for the human race. Unlike the apes, or the scientists on the moon, he is *ready* because he has reached a point from which turning back is practically impossible, and the old parameters can no longer contain his psyche. So on his journey through the Star Gate, he is dying like a caterpillar dies, and it's terrifying. But it will be okay. Now, I might be the first to admit that applying "okay" to the rebirth of the human race that forms the climax of *2001* is an understatement (of the kind early in the movie when someone hopes that a speech about the possible imminent destruction of the human race will be a "morale booster"). But I'm so over-whelmed by the experience of the film that it seems impossible to know the right word. *Evolution? Revolution? Redemption?*

These words are too small, or their meaning has been mis-laid through overuse. But my purpose here is not to encourage you to agree with my interpretation of the film. I want you to watch it because I think that, in dealing with the most profound questions of our existence, *2001* may be the most optimistic film ever made.

In many ways *2001* is the story of the miracle, and the struggle, that each human life always is. Kubrick and Clarke suggest that our destiny may be to evolve into nothing less than the substance of love. Literal analysis may not be most appropriate; it's better to approach *2001* as a meditative text, a fusion of sound and image that can fill your field of vision and stir your heart to consider just what ancient texts might mean when they speak of humans being made "a little lower than the angels."

What "happens," for what it's worth, is this: An astronaut is chosen to travel through and beyond time, becoming the next phase of human evolution. He is childlike, grace-filled, and totally free. In the novel written alongside the film, his first act appears to be the destruction of the world's nuclear weaponry. He's not sure what to do next, but as the novel's last line has it, he "will think of something."

I first saw *2001* as a child, so it has been with me for over forty years. My perception of the film has changed with me. We are to judge ourselves on the basis only of what we know, which must include that there is much that we *don't* know. The film claims to take us "beyond the infinite" and recognizes that there are times when life may feel like we're up against a computer's unblinking eye, just as Bowman is during a large portion of the film. Sometimes we have to live through terrifying things; perhaps these days we may feel that *we* are what happens when the world's mind is going.

But when the glass shatters on the floor in the room where Bowman is waiting to be (re)born, it reminds us that sometimes a sharp break is necessary to initiate the next stage of who we are becoming. The gift of the end sequence of *2001* is the notion of seeing ourselves at all our ages—from today to elderhood (if we're not already there), and then to rebirth. Faced right, this is an invitation to live into our fullest selves, beginning now—an embodiment of the mystic Meister Eckhart's astonishment that "the eye through which I see God is the same eye through which God sees me."

Contemplating the expansiveness of the universe around us, and the universe within, can lead to such initiations. You never know what is or isn't awaiting you. The key is to be willing to surrender to it—to know, with Rilke, that "no feeling is final."

As far as I know, neither Kubrick nor Clarke claimed to believe in God, but they also didn't care much for telling others how to interpret their own work. For me, *2001* is the cinematic embodiment of a newborn baby grasping toward light, or an ancient sage imagining the journey to afterlife. People who live among the dying often tell of moments when the line blurs between earthly existence and beyond. In this light, the idea of purgatory may be a healthy one—not as punishment but as a space of preparing to enter a state un-imaginably different from anywhere you or I have been.

Bowman's journey takes him over a mountainous desert-scape, the point being that we must face our primal side if we are to emerge from the chrysalis that holds us prisoners of our violent animal past. *2001* suggests that we are asleep until God speaks to us, and that being in God's presence is something to be *undergone*, with awe, with gratitude, with surrender. We may think we know things, and we may want certainty about things for which certainty is impossible. But certainty loses its importance beside the confrontation, the sheer *experience* of life itself. A life of fears and loves, in which we are invited to slow down and approach or even enter Spirit, for the sake of . . . how should I put it? Wouldn't you travel as far as Bowman does if you knew it might make you into a *human*?

I wonder if the vision of life lived in the light of eternity (both after and before we got here) requires us to take death as well as birth more seriously, even to make a friend of it. Not in a morbid or self-serving sense. There's something about death that is a lot less fearful than we make it. Perhaps what *2001* tells us is that death shouldn't be so frightening after all—because in being born, we've already died once.

We could spend the rest of our lives meditating on the simple fact of our own birth. Where did we come from, how were we made, what did we come into? What might it be like, at any age, to hold gently a vision of ourselves, growing in the womb, emerging into light for which our eyes weren't ready, landing in a family that may have provided warmth, or only partial shelter, or none at all? No matter what the circumstances of your life today, you were once tiny and helpless. You once had to face ordeals you could not under-stand and were offered gifts that you did not know what to do with. You were born bloodstained and screaming. You are a universe. And a miracle.

Kathleen

It may seem absurd for Gareth to claim that the film *2001* is a metaphor for pregnancy. Not only does the film have no significant female characters but most of it takes place in the sterile white interior of a spaceship. No blood, no messy afterbirth. While metaphor has its place, women know that the rigors of pregnancy and childbirth are all too real, as their bodies are beset by visible bodily changes along with raging hormones, before and after a baby is born.

I've never been pregnant, but I have plenty of family members and friends who've shared their experiences, and I've held bowls for women suffering from morning sickness as they vomited up their breakfasts. Women tell me that the pain of childbirth is terrible but that it quickly fades from memory once they are holding a beloved newborn in their arms. Enduring pregnancy and childbirth strikes me as the epitome of courage, as women are willingly giving birth to a person who will one day die.

And that does connect us with Stanley Kubrick's film—and why reading it as a metaphor for pregnancy is so insightful. As Gareth says, birth *is* a kind of death, and we begin dying the moment we're born. But we're happy to ignore that, as we should, in celebrating the coming of a new human being into the world. *2001* is about humans coming into the world and evolving from inarticulate, prehistoric creatures concerned only with survival to people capable of self-sacrificing love.

I suspect that many moviegoers today, accustomed to the frenetic pace of CGI-fueled action flicks, would find *2001* ponderous and boring, as did many moviegoers and reviewers upon its release in 1968. But here, Gareth's suggestion of the pregnancy metaphor might help. Women wait out a pregnancy knowing that their delivery date is a rough guess; a baby will emerge when it is ready. Kubrick and Clarke remind us that there's a lot of waiting on a decades-long voyage to a distant planet, and Kubrick is determined to make us feel it, even if we resist. Ironically, as this is a film set in the technology-driven world of space exploration, its pace is that of rural life. Nothing can be hurried on a farm: you plant a seed and wait for it to sprout. Nothing can be hurried in pregnancy either: like farming or gardening, it returns us to the basic, slow, sure processes of life.

But from an early age most of us reject slow and steady. Picture a crowded physician's waiting room. A little boy fidgets and whines as his mother explains that it's not yet their turn to see the doctor, that others are ahead of them. When he loudly protests, "But I don't *like* to wait!" adults in the room smile. The boy is expressing something they feel but are not free to say aloud.

Learning to wait is part of growing up, leaving the self-centered world of childhood and entering one in which other people may matter more than ourselves. When we grow exasperated over waiting, it can help to consider Catherine of Siena's admonition that our impatience is the marrow of pride.[1]

We can always refuse to wait and choose to be fully present in the present moment. That sort of wisdom is epitomized in a pregnant woman. Both father and mother are described as "expectant," but it's the mother who experiences drastic changes in her body. Eventually she feels another life stirring and kicking inside her, and soon she will not be able to look down and see her feet. She may feel as untethered from the earth as an astronaut on a space walk. And still, she waits.

I'm glad I saw *2001* when it was first released. Gareth is correct in saying that no one had seen anything like it before. Today it feels contemporary and even futuristic. But emerging from the theater into Honolulu's dazzling sunlight in 1968 was a shock. It was as if I had truly spent the last few hours in the dark of space and had to reorient myself to this world. I suspect that my disorientation, like the experience of being born, was exactly what Kubrick intended.

Kubrick and Clarke were wise to use a symbol rather than something more literal to represent an alien being. The black monolith that appears to the early apelike creatures and influences them to make tools and weapons is later found buried on the moon by a more tech-savvy human race. They determine that it has been buried there for four million years. As men in spacesuits approach, it emits a piercing alarm, alerting the culture from which it came that the earth creatures are now advanced enough to have left their planet and discovered it.

Seeing *2001* now, I marvel that so many of the things that thrilled me in 1968 still please me. The bone used as a weapon by a primitive human and tossed into the air that suddenly becomes a satellite orbiting the earth. The stately Strauss waltzes that seem oddly appropriate for the sight of giant vessels lumbering through space. The woman wearing boots that keep her from floating in a gravity-free environment who walks upside down to deliver trays of food to people on another deck. And a traveler pondering lengthy directions for using a zero-gravity toilet.

When the film abruptly shifts to a large spaceship that is being sent as a probe to Jupiter, the place from which the monolith's signal has come, we meet two astronauts, young scientists who are dull and matter-of-fact in their demeanor and conversation. HAL, the computer that controls all the systems on the ship, is more interesting. But HAL's focus on the mission, even at the expense of the humans on board, has tragic consequences.

This soon does not matter, because after one of the two men dies, the alien intelligence takes hold of the other and changes him utterly. His fate reminds me of something a four-year-old child once told me. She found God in everything, especially in the wonders of creation. She was convinced that before she was born, she had lived among the stars.

Her instinct is true. The ending of *2001* is no more or less mysterious than what the theoretical physicist Lawrence Krauss once said about the origins of humanity: "Every atom in your body came from a star. The atoms in your left hand probably came from a different star than your right hand. It really is the most poetic thing I know about physics: You are all stardust."[2]

2001: A Space Odyssey suggests that the stars are in our future as well as our past. So slow down and enjoy the ride.

Questions and Conversations

1. Who loved you into being (even if you might have never met them)?
2. What effect did your birth have on other people?
3. What were the background noises of the period leading up to your birth? What was happening politically and culturally in your society and the wider world? What was happening in your immediate and extended family?
4. What good things have taken the longest to emerge in your life, and which were the most worth waiting for?

5. Early in *2001*, when the bone thrown in the air cuts
   to the spacecraft, it symbolizes both technological
   progress and the initiation of a world being born.
   What are some examples of such initiation in your
   life?

2

CHILDHOOD

What Maisie Knew (USA/Canada/Netherlands, 2012)
Directed by Scott McGehee and David Siegel, written by Carroll
Cartwright and Nancy Doyne (from the novel by Henry James)

A rare example of older literature being updated for the screen
while retaining the texture of the original, *What Maisie Knew* is
heartrending, though not hopeless. Maisie's parents are tearing each other apart without recognizing that their tug of war
has Maisie at its center. The interaction of unresolved wounds
infecting an adult's capacity for truly loving a child, along
with the child's natural capacity for wonder and resilience,
gives way finally to a form of reconciliation by departure, and
embrace by setting free.

Kathleen

What Maisie Knew can be difficult to watch if you care about
children and understand what they need from the adults
around them. One of the saddest things I have ever heard is

21

what a friend with five siblings said of her parents: "They're two people who never should have had children." She could have been speaking of Maisie's parents: Susanna, played by Julianne Moore, and Beale, played by Steve Coogan. Mom's a self-important, fading rock star; Dad's an international art dealer who pretends to be more successful than he is. They're two unhappy people who reflexively inflict their pain on those around them: the mother overtly, in loud flashes of rage, the father in a more guarded fashion, hiding behind a comic mask.

In the 1897 novel on which this film is based, Henry James notes that in fighting over custody of their young daughter, Maisie's parents had "abandoned [her] to her fate. What was clear to any spectator," he writes, "was this lamentable fact of her being a ready vessel for bitterness, a deep little porcelain cup in which biting acids could be mixed." Her parents "had wanted her not for any good they could do her, but for the harm they could, with her unconscious aid, do each other."[1] Today, as in the nineteenth century, it's not unusual to see parents using custody battles as an opportunity to settle scores.

Children are so vulnerable because they accept the world they are given. Maisie's innocence is inspiring, but she is also an observant six-year-old surviving in a household in which bickering is the constant background noise. While Dad shouts, "I've had my midlife crisis; you should get on with yours," and Mom responds with an obscenity, Maisie knows to ignore them and help Margo, the au pair, by running to get cash for the "pizza man" when he rings the doorbell of their luxurious multilevel apartment. She even knows how much to tip. Maisie seems thoughtful and wise beyond her years, and the look of resignation on her face when her parents break their promises or tell her things no child should have to hear is heartbreaking.

Maisie's parents not only use their child to strike at each other; they use others in the same way. After their inevitable separation, her father suddenly marries Margo; in response, Mom marries Lincoln, a handsome, good-natured hanger-on in her entourage. Neither is a love match: the appeal of these two young people is apparently that they can provide free childcare. And they do their best. One night Maisie is running a fever and needs rest instead of being shuttled to the chaotic environment of her mom's apartment, because the custody agreement specifies that it's her night there. Lincoln says that Susanna will be angry if he returns without Maisie, but Margo appeals to his common sense: "She's a child; she's not well," words that come as a breath of fresh air.

It's tempting to romanticize childhood as a carefree time, but any teacher can tell you that many children arrive in their classrooms with the weight of the world—or at least their dysfunctional families—on their small shoulders. We need the relief of seeing Maisie giggling with other children at school, throwing herself into art projects, and playing basketball. But it's painful to see her try to make sense of the changing relationships of the adults around her. How can she begin to comprehend Susanna's bitter description of Margo as "a tramp with a daddy fixation"? And when Lincoln arrives at school one afternoon to pick up Maisie, it is clear she doesn't know that this man she's seen in passing at home has just married her mother. Susanna has not told her. Lincoln tells a startled teacher, "I'm her new stepfather," but admits that "she doesn't really know who I am."

Later, at home, sitting on her mother's lap, Maisie asks her if she really married Lincoln. Susanna replies, "Yes, but I still love you best." We wince when Susanna whispers in her ear, "I married him for you," and are not surprised that Susanna grows jealous when Lincoln and Maisie begin to develop a bond. Lincoln has helped Maisie draw a castle with a moat and drawbridge, and Susanna clearly feels ignored while Maisie reads the report on castles that she's prepared for school. "What am I? Invisible?" she whines and snaps at Lincoln, saying in front of Maisie, "You don't get a bonus for making her fall in love with you." At moments like these the film can feel like a manual on how not to raise a child. But it can also cause us to think about how we relate to children and how we can choose a way that is better for them and for us.

We see Maisie weep only once, when her mother's carelessness creates a cascade of mishaps that make it seem that everyone in her life has abandoned her. Waking confused to find herself in a stranger's apartment, Maisie says, plaintively, "I want to go home." We're relieved when Margo arrives to take her there, and relieved also to find that unlike the child in James's novel, Maisie is not abandoned. Margo and Lincoln offer genuine affection, and Maisie's response to them reassures me about what it is that she knows. While Maisie loves her mother and father, she also understands that they are ill-equipped to provide the love and attention she deserves. What Maisie endures cuts me to the heart, and while she accepts the incomprehensible and sometimes cruel remarks of careless adults, she knows it's important to soak up love when it is offered.

I have worked as a kindergarten aide and have long been interested in how children develop their sense of how the world works. It amazes me that we all start out as infants with only the most basic physical instincts, but within a year or two, we are stringing words together to communicate with others. But responsible parents learn to listen to their children even when they're preverbal. I was once watching a grand-niece who was seventeen months old, happily playing with toys, and lifting them one by one for me to admire. Suddenly, for no apparent reason, she began to wail. Her mother called from the kitchen, "That's her water cry. She wants her water bottle." I went to fetch it, and as I handed it to the child, she accepted it with surprise, her expression indicating that she felt I wasn't as stupid as I looked. It made my day.

This experience reminded me that parenthood is relentlessly demanding. It requires not only paying attention but making sacrifices that people as self-absorbed as Susanna and Beale are unwilling or unable to make. Susanna is like a child inhabiting the body of an adult, using her daughter as a playmate and confidante, and confusing this for love. She's unable to recognize how unfair this is to Maisie.

The abuse that Maisie's parents dish out is all too familiar, if you listen to what exasperated parents say to their children. It's even more lamentable for being largely unconscious. This film is a wake-up call, not only for parents but for all of us, to remember that from infancy, children are people and deserve respect as well as love. In my experience, too many adults fail to comprehend how deeply children ponder serious issues. Psychologists have discovered that children develop a moral sense long before they can talk. In one experiment they provided a puppet show to babies and toddlers in which one puppet was notably mean to the other puppets. After the show, when the children were invited to play with the puppets, they consistently rejected the mean puppet. The psychologists repeated the experiment, switching the role of the cruel puppet so that it was clear the children were not responding to facial features or the colors of the puppet's hair or clothing but were recognizing cruel behavior. Children as young as fifteen months old refused to interact with a puppet that had been mean.

Maisie knows that her parents' behavior toward each other, and toward her, is not good. She has adapted and refuses to judge them. But she has also learned to stand up for herself. After Maisie has spent several happy days at a beach cottage with Margo and Lincoln, her mother appears unexpectedly and asks Maisie to join her on the last leg of a tour, enticing her by telling her she has gifts for her on the bus. When Maisie refuses to leave, Susanna whines, asking, "You know I'm your mother, right?" Maisie nods but stands firm.

The last image of this film is a marvel, a fleeting but powerful moment. It's the next morning, and Margo and Lincoln are keeping a promise they have made to Maisie. She cannot contain her excitement as she runs down a dock to the small boat whose owner has offered to take the three of them for a ride at sea. The expression on her face is a mix of dreaminess and determination, joy and liberation. It's the smile of a child who is finally free to be of no use to anyone but just a happy little girl.

Gareth

The Belfast poet Michael Longley says that poetry is of "no use, but that doesn't mean . . . it has no value."[2] I think I know what he means, but I think all art forms can indeed be "useful"—especially when loneliness is mirrored, love affirmed, or injustice exposed. (*Oliver Twist* motivated aristocratic women to help end the monstrosity of the Victorian workhouse, and Krzysztof Kieślowski's film *A Short Film about Killing* helped end the death penalty in Poland.) I suspect Longley means a different use—that poetry doesn't need to have measurable outcomes. What it "does" for us should not be the question; the fact of its existence is enough.

If that's true of a poem, how much more so a person? I was struck by Kathleen's comment that Maisie is free to be of no use to anyone. What the world would be if we didn't see one another as people to be used. To be a child is to be vulnerable, of course, and in need of protection, but being a child should also mean to be allowed curiosity and wonder. Ideal parents set their children free (within safe parameters) to explore, learn, and feel. Such parents know that, as the philosopher Alan Watts put it, "Everybody is I."³ But there are no ideal parents or ideal situations, just invitations to decide what to do with what we have been given and to make it more like a dream—or a nightmare.

A dream it would be if everybody truly *saw* everybody else's "I"—if all adults treated children as individuals worthy of respect and age-appropriate autonomy and loved them just because they are. I once daydreamed about the creation of the world while looking out at a Wyoming lake and the surrounding mountains. If I had made the world as good as this Wyoming lake and mountains, never mind the lakes of Malawi or the mountains of Tibet, I might enjoy it for a few eons, say. But a time would come when I wanted to share it. And if I knew how to make people, I might do just that.

I might then realize that forcing people to do my bidding would make them robots and not souls. I would have to let them choose for themselves—and accept the danger that they might not turn out the way I want. They would face struggles and grief as well as ease and delight. They might think well of me, or they might not love me back. But if I loved them *just because they are*, they might come to see that life does not have to be a competition for either affection or success. They might come to believe that everybody is I, and therefore all we need do is to bring what we have and ask for what we need.

I had a therapist who referred to the average boyhood as "an emotional genocide." An overstatement, but I understood: he was describing the tearing and breaking of the spirit, the oppressive gender and social role essentialism, the messages of "you'll never amount to anything," the pressure to fight to be seen or heard in the world. These experiences are all too common across lines of gender, class, race, and culture.

But there is also the gift of claiming childlikeness as an adult, of healing the one within who was previously brutalized in body or spirit. There's a reason that spiritual wisdom traditions speak of childlikeness as the pathway to enlightenment. Not *childishness* but rather a life-affirming rejection of cynicism, giving ourselves to the spirit that responds to catastrophe by planting trees. Think of Desmond Tutu's infectious joy amid terrible suffering. Knowing the people were well aware of their pain, he also knew they needed a vision of possibility.

So I am grateful for *What Maisie Knew*, for honoring childhood as a place to which we can return in our minds (if it was whole) or heal from (where it was broken) so that we can experience, right now, the power of loving ourselves, just because we are.

▲▼▲

I don't know about you, but I can still be triggered back into childhood, scared of some "grown-ups," scared of the boys at school, scared of the world. Yet sometimes I also seem to be older than I am. I can project myself into an imagined future as a wise elder. Such imagination is pieced together from faces I've seen and stories I've read—some from my lived experience, like my grandmother and my friend Terry, and some from cinema, like Lillian Gish's warrior-grandmother in *The Night of the Hunter* (another great film about childhood, one which knows that sometimes kids are braver than the adults around them) or Bill Cobbs's portrayal of a wry guardian angel in *The Hudsucker Proxy*. Sometimes I sense someone wiser than me trying to be born from within.

In *What Maisie Knew*, Onata Aprile gives one of the great performances by a child actor. Pushed around by insecure grown-ups who can't grow up, she's a victim of villagelessness who can't experience the consolations of community because she doesn't have one, or the one she does have is full of holes. When people hate each other as much as her parents do, it poisons everything; a quiet meal is impossible, a stress-free playdate, unthinkable.

What Maisie knows can't be underestimated, but she will need an adult mind to help her process it. It's no wonder that the grown-ups who show her the most care are the ones most in touch with their own vulnerabilities. Her parents are addicted to commerce: one selling art (one of the strangest distortions of reality: the trading of creative works, made to be seen but often gathering dust in vaults, only to be traded again), the other selling an onstage image. Her accidental guardians don't have the luxury of worrying about reputation. They live from paycheck to paycheck, don't have the security of being named on their own apartment lease, and are realizing that being in love with someone who cares more about status than people means they will always come second.

The first step of Alcoholics Anonymous is to admit powerlessness, that we are unable to heal ourselves by ourselves. One lesson of *What Maisie Knew*, beyond the obvious one of not abandoning a little one unable to fend for herself, is that to put your own oxygen mask on first requires the humility to accept that there are some places you can't breathe unaided. With wisdom we might recognize our childhood wounds, might even see that the gift is in the wound, might even turn the wound into a scar, and witness the scar becoming a source of medicine.

Before we can do that, there is separation, descent, and ordeal. We must experience abandonment before we can be found. *What Maisie Knew* trusts that no one in the audience is without a story of abandonment, or one of doing the abandoning. But in how it sees Maisie, the movie says that even if you never were the apple of anybody else's eye, or even if you merely never knew you were, you can still become your own treasure. Maisie observes and is touched and wounded by the world, but her resilience never suffocates her wonder. "Let's go on a boat," she says; her guardians want to make it happen because they love her but also because they want to be reminded of what it is to be cared for too. Her toys teach her how to be, to tend to the "needs" of a doll, to experiment with different "voices" until we find the one that is truly ours. She, like we, can be okay.

But we won't be healed, or tended, or caressed by the world if the only world we know is made from money and power. There are villages to be made, even in cities, and they must be, for we were not made to live as machines. (One of the marvelous grace notes of this film is how it shows that architecture and built environments can leave us alternately hemmed in or liberated into possibility.) The question is if we will even see the *possibility* of making a village, wherever we are, never mind the *necessity*.

What Maisie Knew is shorter than many movies, but it's perfectly formed. It knows that many of us grew up hearing our parents fight and that it is difficult for some of us to find love that lasts or helps us transcend our selfishness. Here children are treated like adults—or abandoned to their fate like adults—and adults act like badly behaved children. Yet

Maisie loves unconditionally, learns to look after a turtle, and may even one day learn to look after herself.

What Maisie Knew is an artistic cousin to any tale about adults who, unconscious of their impact on others, haven't turned their wounds into scars. But then, a miracle: in *What Maisie Knew* one grown-up finally behaves like one, remembering how she used to feel before she even knew that growing up was possible. The key to being a truly integrated adult may well be to remember what it is like to be a child.

Questions and Conversations

Thinking about childhood can be painful, even traumatic. So in discussing *What Maisie Knew*, be tender with yourself and others—listen carefully for the resonances with other people's stories and for the possibility of assisting each other on the way, to hold gently the fact that while we may not be able to change the past of a painful childhood, the invitation to become childlike and experience wonder at any age is always available to us.

1. What is one of the best lessons you remember about your childhood?
2. What is your earliest memory of your parents?
3. How would you describe your parents' understanding of you as a child, teenager, young or not-so-young adult?
4. What does Maisie know?
5. If you could live one perfect day as a child, what would it be?
6. What's stopping you from living that same day now?

7. How could you, in the next week, help a child experience wonder? Perhaps more importantly, how could you help yourself?

8. There's no overt mention of God, religion, or church in *What Maisie Knew*, but the movie clearly demonstrates the effect that genuine, unconditional love can have on a child. How do you connect your understanding of such love with your image of God?

3

COMMUNITY

The Seventh Fire (USA, 2015)

Directed by Jack Riccobono, written by Jack Riccobono, Shane Omar Slattery-Quintanilla, and Andrew Ford

> On an Ojibwe reservation in Minnesota, two men face trouble with the law as they struggle to build better lives.

Smoke Signals (USA/Canada, 1998)

Directed by Chris Eyre, written by Sherman Alexie

> The first movie to be written, directed, coproduced, and acted by Native Americans, about two young men going on a road trip of grief and acceptance.

Kathleen

I once gave the commencement address at South Dakota State University and was glad to see that a pole representing traditional Native American spirituality, with feathers and medicine pouches, was on the dais. But as the students came forward to receive their diplomas, I was distressed to see so few Indigenous young people among them. The university works hard to attract Native students and offers many programs to encourage them to stay. When I told a professor what I had observed during the ceremony, he said, "For many of them, the pull of the reservation is too strong; they can't bear to live apart from their communities."

Community is a basic human need. For most of us family is our first community, and parents know that their children need to socialize and form new communities at school, religious institutions, or on sports teams. A big part of transitioning from adolescence to adulthood is finding communities in which we feel free to be ourselves, respected and loved for who we are. People tend to form transitory communities when the need arises, during natural disasters, or when they're stranded for hours at an airport waiting out a storm. Assistance is offered, life stories are exchanged, and confessions are made that might be easier to share with strangers than with friends or family.

Community has special meaning for Benedictine men and women as they welcome into their monasteries candidates from a wide variety of backgrounds and must help them grow into people who will place the group's needs over their own. In our individualistic society this is a tall order, and the process takes about seven years. At a time when people are reluctant to make lifelong commitments, it is inspiring to see how the young learn from the old in a monastery and vice versa. They have promised to remain with and support each other until death, and this allows deep, intergenerational bonds of friendship to develop that strengthen the community.

In their 1,500 years of existence, Benedictines have learned that community does not happen by accident. It requires deliberation and perseverance. But it's remarkable to see what ensues when a person is determined to create a community in an unlikely setting. I live in a condominium with 136 units, an ordinary apartment building, except that our resident manager encourages everyone to get to know their neighbors. It's catching on: now when people are moving in, I welcome them to the building. Some people don't respond, but I have found that most are glad to talk about where they came from and what drew them to the neighborhood. And community proves its worth in a crisis: when a malfunctioning drain in my apartment caused flooding on my floors, neighbors were quick to come with sponges and mops to help me clear the mess.

Community is of vital importance for people in close-knit ethnic groups and Indigenous tribes. Without it they can become lost. In the early 1950s, the American government's Bureau of Indian Affairs (BIA) launched a "voluntary relocation program" to get Native Americans off reservations and move them to cities where they could be assimilated into American society. I have a childhood memory of one family from a South Dakota reservation who came to Waukegan, Illinois, where my family then lived. My dad was the choir director at a Congregational church that had offered to assist the family. One church member had found the father a job at Abbott Laboratories. Someone donated a used car, and others provided furniture for their rented house. Their rent was to be subsidized by the government for several months.

My parents, who were raised in South Dakota, invited the family to dinner. My brother and I played with the children; our family dog seemed glad to have new kids to chase around the yard. I had heard my father say that the relocation program made no sense, and I'm certain that he knew this family was miserable in Illinois and longed to go home.

When the family suddenly returned to South Dakota, leaving not long after that dinner, many in the church felt that they had been ungrateful. But my parents noted that trying to "help" Indigenous people by severing them from their roots, their culture, and their community was not only foolish but a recipe for disaster.

The relocation program's stated goal was to integrate Indigenous people into mainstream American society. But the aim of many BIA leaders was to erase Native culture entirely. People who had lived off the land, farming, fishing, and hunting in traditional communities, became isolated, working low-wage jobs and subsisting in urban slums. This created a trauma whose effects are still being felt by Native people today. I believe it's behind the reluctance of many young people to remain at South Dakota State University, because they fear that being there puts them in danger of losing their community and their identity.

It's good to see that after years of Native Americans being stereotyped and misrepresented in film, often portrayed by white actors wearing "red face," Indigenous novelists, screenwriters, and directors are producing works that reflect life as it's lived by Natives today. Their resistance to romanticizing the "noble savage" is neatly summed up by the great Indigenous actor Graham Greene's response to a white director who had once asked him to "Stand there and look stoic." Greene replied, "I'll do that, if you stand there and look stupid."

Smoke Signals (1998), directed by Chris Eyre, with a screenplay by Sherman Alexie based on his short story collection, *The Lone Ranger and Tonto Fistfight in Heaven*, is, for me, the most engaging of these films. Set on Idaho's Coeur d'Alene Reservation, it's suffused with ironic humor: a woman drives a car that will only work in reverse, and a radio DJ announces, "It's a good day to be Indigenous" while turning to the traffic monitor stationed at a rural intersection and reporting, "A big truck just went by."

No stoic symbols here, just two young men, Victor Joseph and Thomas Builds-the-Fire, who have a complicated and strained relationship. Thomas is a dreamer and storyteller enamored of Native spirituality. Victor is more cynical and angry, an impatient man who often becomes exasperated with Thomas, accusing him of getting most of his knowledge of Indigenous tradition from *Dances with Wolves*. But the two men share a bond because Victor's father, Arnold, rescued Thomas as an infant from a house fire that killed his parents.

Victor has bitter childhood memories of Arnold's alcoholism and abuse. He hasn't forgiven him for running away after the fire and abandoning his family. But when he learns that Arnold has died in Arizona, he feels compelled to go there to retrieve his ashes. He and his mother don't have the money for the trip, and Victor is surprised when Thomas offers to cover their expenses if Victor allows him to come along.

Smoke Signals has both classic road trip and coming of age elements, but the film transcends both genres. As the two men come to understand each other, we sense that they're both becoming more adult, more prepared for the information that the woman who has been living with Arnold has to offer. Consumed with guilt over accidentally causing the fatal fire when he was drunk, Arnold—magnificently played by Gary Farmer—had decided that he was a threat to his family and had to leave them and the reservation behind. He stopped drinking and built a new life for himself. As Victor and Thomas decide how to dispose of his ashes and begin the journey home, we realize that the men have experienced a much-needed healing.

Other remarkable films about contemporary Native communities include *Skins*, another Chris Eyre film, based on a novel by Adrian C. Louis, set on South Dakota's Pine Ridge Reservation, and *Powwow Highway*, based on a novel by David Seals, set on the Northern Cheyenne Reservation in Lame Deer, Montana, directed by Jonathan Wacks and produced by George Harrison (also known as a Beatle). What sets these films apart from earlier representations of Native life in cinema is that they offer compelling stories about Native people living in the present and not the past. Their sardonic wit and humor temper the natural bitterness many Natives feel about how badly Native people have always been treated by the newcomers in America. They feature fine performances by well-known actors such as Cardinal, Farmer, and Greene, and younger ones including Evan Adams, Adam Beach, A. Martinez, Lois Red Elk, Joanelle Romero, and Eric Schweig.

But it's a 2015 documentary, *The Seventh Fire*, directed by Jack Pettibone Riccobono and produced by Terrence Malick, that speaks most directly to me about the pitfalls of life in an insular community. Set on the White Earth Reservation in northern Minnesota, whose residents gave the filmmaker extraordinary access, it features Rob Brown, a gang leader and drug dealer who has spent much of his thirty-seven years in prison. He is currently facing his fifth prison term and will leave behind a pregnant girlfriend. His regret for all the violence he's brought to the reservation is amplified by his concern for a teenage protégé, Kevin Fineday, who also has a pregnant girlfriend and seems destined to repeat Rob's mistakes unless he can get off drugs and abandon his dream of becoming the reservation's crime boss.

Rob's troubled past includes a series of foster homes from which he ran away, committing petty crimes as a juvenile that soon led to more serious ones. He has a daughter in third grade and clearly wants better things for her. Kevin's girlfriend hopes he'll settle down, but he struggles to find a job and is lured by the easy money found in dealing cocaine and meth. Both men seek healing by reconnecting with the spiritual traditions of their tribe.

But scenes of women casually cutting dope on a kitchen table in front of their young children make you realize how normalized drugs have become on the reservation and why Kevin says that the only way he can get clean is to leave. He observes that few people, maybe one every ten years, have succeeded in making a life for themselves off the reservation, in what he calls "the real world." But he struggles to remain in a rehab center, and its director, Albino Garcia, tells Kevin that he needs to be willing to get sober. Both Garcia and Rob believe that culture and community can heal, and as the film ends, we see a photo of Rob as a boy, dressed in traditional clothing to dance at a powwow. But it's difficult to maintain much hope for him, Kevin, or their children.

The film's reception does bring some hope. Selected to screen at the White House in March 2016 as part of President Obama's campaign for criminal justice reform, it was followed by a panel discussion. Both Rob and Kevin participate, along with Troy Molloy, a Chippewa who serves as a liaison between the Department of Justice and Native tribes, and Karen Diver, a White House adviser on Native affairs, who had been elected the tribal chief on Minnesota's Fond du Lac Reservation.

All have experience battling stereotypes of drugged or drunken Native people, and Diver said she was worried that the film would perpetuate them. But the scene of Rob consulting with an attorney and reading aloud his history of childhood abandonment, foster homes, and extensive rap sheet convinced her that the film could instruct people about the failure of the American justice system to address the mental illness that arises out of continued trauma. Rob's downward spiral might have been checked if someone had recognized early how troubled he was and provided him with counseling and treatment. But for many reasons—poverty, lack of resources, and untreated trauma—his community could not do that.

Rob says that since he was released from prison, writing has helped him find a voice and he hopes to use it to help members of his community. Kevin went to prison shortly after the film was completed, and since his release he has been trying to help others avoid making the bad choices that got him into trouble.

An audience member mentions a comment Kevin makes early in the film about feeling overwhelmed by hopelessness and the sense that his community would never change. She asks how he feels about that now. He replies that the town has changed for the worse; children as young as nine are now using and dealing drugs. He had to leave the reservation to save himself. Kevin adds that he never expected to be invited to speak at the White House and makes one comment that illustrates how different his world is from that of middle-class Americans. This trip was his first airplane ride and first trip outside Minnesota.

Gareth

As a child in northern Ireland, I heard about "two communities," Catholic-Irish and Protestant-British, but I didn't identify with either.[1] My family's mixed heritage left me unsure where I belonged. Many folks didn't feel safe to share too much about themselves, so the idea of a community seemed to belong to other people. But I wanted it so much. I lived vicariously through movies about people living together, looking after each other. Loneliness is a killer, and community the antidote, although the most whole communities also honor and make space for the inner life. Isolation and contemplation are not the same thing, which is partly why wise elders are often found on the outskirts (literally and metaphorically), but they're not hiding. There they lead examined lives, with open doors, but also know when to close them. Two men in *The Seventh Fire* appear to be this kind of elder. One offers Kevin support but also holds boundaries when he crosses them, and the other is Albino Garcia, founder of La Plazita Institute, where culture does indeed heal.

The Seventh Fire is a challenging and painful story, one not immediately obvious as a portal into exploring community. There's also a risk in using a story about the underbelly of a marginalized community, especially when the cinematic treatment of Native American people has so often been dehumanizing. But *The Seventh Fire* loves people and respects suffering, and it doesn't need to explicitly evoke colonization and genocide to ask how things got so bad for these people and what must happen next. *Smoke Signals* is tonally warmer, a treasure of a film, but it also points to how community often forms in response to pain, pressure, and scarcity. Perhaps we are all "children born of flame and ash," as one of the protagonists says, looking for a hearth that can hold both.

Early in *The Seventh Fire*, Kevin goes looking for a little lost girl, anxious for her safety. He's doing what community is for, and he's showing something that should be obvious but may be unnoticed. Community does not just happen—it takes somebody to begin it. Once it's underway, it takes somebody to repeat it, to pass on traditions and to facilitate the ways in which community will continue. As when Kristine, Rob's ex-girlfriend, swaddles her newborn, there must have been a time when humans figured out that babies needed to be cozily wrapped in order to adjust to life outside the womb. Whoever learned that passed it on. Community depends on it.

▲▼▲

Many movies deal with community, but I'll mention just two here. *The Godfather* presents a kind of community that draws the boundaries too tightly, focusing on its own survival rather than the common good. A community defined by who it excludes is a prison. There is life-giving contrast in my favorite movie about community: *Smoke* (1995, directed by Wayne Wang and Paul Auster). Set around a Brooklyn cigar store, it has a physical hub, an elder (in the form of the store manager), and eventually a purpose bigger than itself: reaching out to help someone in need results in the expansion of the community. *Smoke* is one of those lovely films that helps me feel less alone just by watching it, and it gives a model for community to aspire to.

The best communities are not just a safety net in times of trouble but also help prevent the trouble in the first place. They are places where trust is deepened among folks who have known each other a long time and who model that trust for the new people, who will always be welcome at the table. They are places where your pain is welcome.

It sounds like Kathleen's condo building is such a place—and the manager an elder, encouraging a welcome to new residents. He knows that for community to exist, someone needs to begin it.

1. What community has sustained you in your life, in childhood, young adulthood, and now?
2. What are the most positive and the most negative aspects of belonging to a community?
3. Have you ever felt trapped in a community, sensing that in order to discover and live as your true self you would have to leave?
4. What would a week in the life of your ideal community look and feel like?
5. What's one need you have that could be healed in the culture of a good community?
6. If you're part of a group that has historically been oppressed, has a sense of community helped you cope with trauma?
7. What's one gift you could bring to help nurture the culture of a good community?
8. How could you help initiate more community where you are?

4

THE BREAKING AND REMAKING OF SELF

A friend may well be reckoned the masterpiece of nature.

—Ralph Waldo Emerson

Vocation is the place where our deep gladness meets the world's deep need.

—Frederick Buechner

The Fisher King (USA, 1991)
Directed by Terry Gilliam, written by Richard LaGravenese

A shock jock in love with himself unwittingly goads someone into a mass shooting. In the aftermath of the tragedy, two men find that they need each other to heal each other, while the women they love need them to grow up.

Gareth

Terry Gilliam and Richard LaGravenese's exquisite fantasy is set in New York in the early 1990s, when the city was still grungy enough to feel around every corner the risk of possibility, of threat or wonder. It's a hero's journey in which one of the key things discovered by the hero is that there are no heroes. Or perhaps that we are all invited to heroism, and nobody's part in that is less important than anyone else's.

Robin Williams is Parry, a former professor radically traumatized by the murder of his beloved ("radically" because it has taken him back to something primitive: desperate vulnerability and incapacity to protect himself or ask for help, but also childlike wonder and a dream of salvation). He believes that finding the Holy Grail will save him from a terrorizing Red Knight. This may be as good a metaphor for unintegrated trauma as the movies have delivered.

Jeff Bridges is Jack, a shock jock radio host who is amplifying a purgatory where the vocabulary sounds like the demonic child of the *National Enquirer* and Dorothy Parker. His job entails dehumanization plus stirring up rage with a side of eloquence. At the beginning of the movie, he is so full of himself that he can't see the prison of his own fame. "Thank God I'm me!" he declares, but we beg to differ. For the "me" that he is represents only selfishness, rage, and a lack of accountability.

Practicing the catchphrase for an upcoming TV show intended to make him even more famous—the phrase being "Forgive me!"—Jack unwittingly names what he needs most.

He also notices that the transition from radio to television means that, for the first time in his life, "I'll be a voice *with* a body." While he is indeed about to experience a transition, it's not from semi-famous to really famous. He's going to go on a journey inside himself. This is indeed about becoming a voice with a body. He's going to learn the deeper meaning of the *Pinocchio* motif that shows up in the movie: deception doesn't begin with the lies we tell other people but the ones we tell ourselves. Only when we begin to truly own our story can we write the end of it.

As it turns out, the story Jack is unconsciously living makes him complicit in the mass shooting that took Parry's spouse and mind. Three years later, Jack is broken, borderline homeless, and lazily inattentive to his job as a video store clerk. He's so guilt-ridden and depressed that he does not notice the self-sacrificing love offered by storeowner Anne (Mercedes Ruehl), who isn't asking for much. Just to be seen that she's there, which is the opposite dilemma to Lydia (Amanda Plummer), a nervous and kind young woman who is actually scared to be seen. Perhaps because she was seen before by people who hurt her; probably because she's too kind to fight back.

LaGravenese's script ensures that Anne and Lydia are fully rounded characters, not merely ciphers in service to the men. And despite Ruehl being awarded a richly deserved Oscar for Best Supporting Actress, there are actually four *leads* in this movie. Add a beautiful and heartbreaking supporting performance from the brilliant Michael Jeter, who died too young, like the friends of whom his character speaks, and this is one of the great ensembles.

▲▼▲

Now to the quest. We all have one. The problem is, at least, threefold: many of us never discover the quest; among those who do, many vacillate between self-improvement and selfish ambition; and for those who discover their true calling to service, there's the individualism of our culture to overcome. We all have a quest, but it was never supposed to be pursued alone.

The first step on achieving the quest is called *the separation*—from false certainties: the world of home and reputation and whatever else you tell yourself will save you. There's a reason we call money and status *trappings*. They keep us from finding our true selves. Separation requires stepping away from the things that keep us numb and *throwing* away our crutches. In *The Fisher King*, Jack is separated from his self-righteousness, Parry from his sanity, Anne from her dream that life would work out okay, Lydia from other people.

Then there follows *the descent*, where we meet the shadow, the things we hide, repress, and deny about ourselves—not just the unpleasant stuff but the gifts we conceal out of unhealthy humility or because no one has ever awakened our gifts through initiation and mentoring. By the third scene of *The Fisher King*, Jack is in a hell of his own making, Parry is living in a literal underworld, Anne is asking, "Is that all there is?" and Lydia is on the fringes of everything.

After the descent comes *the ordeal*, where the struggle is most intense. For Parry this has included the most horrifying violence. For Jack the struggle is within—inside his ego, first broken by losing his reputation; then struggling to stay alive, or to get out of bed in the morning, ashamed of what he did and envious of what he no longer has; then resisting the call to get up and do something for others. Breaking into someone's house to steal a cup is the least of his challenges. Breaking free from the prison of selfishness is the real ordeal.

And then *the homecoming*. Some cultures celebrate the return of newly initiated people with dancing, food, lovemaking, and fires lit to mark the auspicious moment and to inspire the next candidates for emotional maturity. More long-lasting is a homecoming to *the self*, the newly calibrated way of being, no longer *broken* but *broken in*. The meek shall inherit the earth, apparently, but *meek* may not mean what most of us have thought. Some people think it refers to what happens to a wild horse after being broken in; it still has the capacity to kick, but it won't. A meeked person would be one who knows how to use a sword but refuses, unless it is necessary to protect the vulnerable from greater harm. A meeked Jack is able to find his charisma again, and might even return to his gift of public storytelling, only this time he won't use it to hurt people. And a meeked Parry has come through the ordeal of horror, reintegrating his psyche with the support of friends and knowing that now it is okay for him to truly grieve. They come home to each other, to the women whom they love and who love them, but most of all, they come home to themselves.

△▽△

So what does *The Fisher King* do for me? Or to me? Or maybe even *through* me? Aside from the delightfully moving performances; the new spaces that Gilliam and his crew make out of a city we thought we knew (and the new light that Roger Pratt's cinematography brings to it); the gorgeous, heart-stopping cameo from Jeter; the brilliant paradox of a suicide attempt thwarted by a murder attempt; the Chinese restaurant scene; and the transcendent Grand Central Station dance sequence evoking the truth that magic is possible anywhere (it may just depend on how you look at things and what you're willing to make of them)—aside from all that, there's also this:

Life is not about what my ego wants for itself, nor some metaphysical blueprint outlining all the twists and turns of one life among billions. Finding my true self is not so much about discovering what I am as *how* I am. It's about how I can dance with my own wounds and the pain of the world, with my own gifts and the opportunity to make a difference—no matter how many people see me. It's about going deep within to discover a mission of service to the common good. That mission begins with discerning our loves—what do we truly care about that can become a place of service to the common good? The rest of life is about figuring out where to put those loves.

Whether it's a terror of things that go bump in the night, or grief at people or hopes lost, they say that while you may never really conquer your demons, perhaps you can learn to live above them. To be aware that they are there but not be ruled by them. Making that kind of life enables us to say, without irony, without arrogance, *Thank God I'm me*. And everyone who knows us will probably agree.

Kathleen

When it comes to using fantastical, over-the-top images to make a point about real life, Terry Gilliam has no equal. But *The Fisher King*, perhaps due in part to an exceptionally thoughtful script by Richard LaGravenese, is a fairly straightforward story about four people who may not even know that they're on a quest to discover their true selves. As Gareth points out, and as the film makes clear, this quest is one that we all share, and we can't do it alone. This film is about love, and it might even be considered a romantic comedy. But it goes deep into considering what love requires of us.

The first character we meet, Jack, is defined by an excessive self-regard. He is a familiar character in our culture, a media personality who knows that the more outrageous his on-air remarks, the more popular his program will be. We get a close-up view of the egotism that fuels Jack's outsized ambition and sense of superiority. To maintain his inflated self-esteem, he needs to demean most of the people who call into his radio show. But when one careless rant causes a disaster that wrecks his career, his fall is a big one. His house of cards collapses and there is nothing at the center but a bitter, cynical shell of a person.

And there's Parry, a traumatized survivor of a horrific act that killed his wife. His grief has become so all-encompassing that it has driven him to madness and caused him to abandon his career and move into a basement boiler room with rats and portraits of medieval knights and ladies, who suggest to him that the answer to his problems lies in engaging in a quest for the Holy Grail. Gareth correctly identifies Parry as suffering from an extreme version of unintegrated trauma, compounded by his inability to ask for the help he needs.

I feel that I know the two women in the film. Anne is smart, with an outgoing, vibrant personality and a lot of love to give. But she's confused self-sacrifice with love and has allowed too many self-absorbed men like Jack to take advantage of her. Only when she recognizes this is she able to break the pattern, begin respecting herself, and start demanding respect from Jack. Will he offer it or not?

Lydia walks as if she is ashamed to be taking up space in the world, cringing from human contact to protect herself from the demands that others place on her. Her mother's regular phone calls always include questions about whether she's found a boyfriend, but Lydia's attempts to date have resulted in dispiriting one-night stands. She has adopted an armor of cynicism regarding relationships with men. But when Parry disarms her after their dinner date by seeking only to kiss her on the cheek and bid her goodnight, we sense that another Lydia, open to being loved, will soon emerge.

Gareth's description of *The Fisher King* as an "exquisite fantasy" is accurate. The film strikes me as a perfect expression of Gilliam's gift for using extremes to reveal basic truths. Its characters are four seriously damaged people, but we would be foolish to dismiss them without considering how much they tell us about our own lives. How do we hide from the demands love makes of us? When did we recognize that our withdrawing from others was a form of narcissism or a fantasy of self-sufficiency? What kind of transitions did we have to undergo in recognizing that we were trying to manipulate and shape people so they could better serve our needs rather than simply love them? These four people may be on a quest to find more honest and fulfilling relationships, but so are we.

It is one mark of Gilliam's genius that he has provided us with a serious film that includes some of the best comedy ever put on film, and it is no surprise that Robin Williams peppers the film with extremely funny remarks. But many unexpected delights linger: the slapstick of noodle-slurping and mayhem with chopsticks in a Chinese restaurant; the appearance, disappearance, and reappearance of a brightly painted Pinocchio doll; and the hilarious use of the song "How about You?" in unlikely settings.

One line sums up the magic of this film for me. Parry wakes from a coma; he has been in a hospital recovering from a brutal assault by thugs who target men they consider worthless bums. Suddenly we realize that much more than physical healing has taken place. Parry says, "I really miss her, Jack—is that okay? Can I miss her now?" and we know that Parry is finally free to love both Lydia and himself. This film might be a balm for anyone who is grieving the loss of someone who was dear to them. Or anyone seeking a deeper understanding of how we are to use our capacity for love to serve one another and the common good.

Questions and Conversations

Considering traumatic memories can be retraumatizing, and it takes a bit of dexterity to reflect on painful matters of the self without opening wounds. *The Spiritual Exercises of St. Ignatius of Loyola* can be instructive here. They invite us to name "sources of consolation and desolation," a more complex method of exploring the everyday question, "How are you doing?" But the *Exercises* don't say, "Let's drown in pain together." Instead, they keep the focus on naming the *sources* of that which is and is not life-giving. So, in discussing the themes raised in *The Fisher King*, we invite you to be gentle with yourself—like you would be with a rare Pinocchio doll. If deeper and more painful issues surface, consider a wise spiritual director or therapist. Medicine people will go on healing the wounded world, and even those who feel they are the most broken can find their own wholeness by helping others.

1. Was there anything you felt you didn't understand?
2. What do each of the four main characters bring to the others?

3. What do each of the four main characters need the most—to let go of and to receive?
4. Which of the four main characters reminded you most of yourself?
5. What do you need to let go of and to receive?
6. What is your quest?
7. What is the next step on your quest?

5

VOCATION—MEANING IN THE ORDINARY

Paterson (USA/Germany/France, 2016)

Directed and written by Jim Jarmusch

Paterson (Adam Driver) is a bus-driving poet and a poet who drives a bus, getting people where they need to go in Paterson, New Jersey, a rundown city with a grand literary tradition. His ordered, quiet life reveals what it can mean to love people selflessly and to create art without egotistic self-indulgence. Paterson loves his wife and is glad to be of service to the strangers who ride his bus. He also writes poems every day. This film has much to say to us about how our society views jobs and vocations. Paterson is an ordinary man who, happily, has found a way to enjoy and fulfill both.

Kathleen

Monks love *Paterson*, and I know why. The film immerses us in the daily routine of a man named Paterson who drives a city bus in Paterson, New Jersey. Portrayed with restraint and sensitivity by Adam Driver, he has adopted a schedule that is as strict as a monastic *horarium*: up at the same early hour every morning, going to work, hearing the same comments and complaints from the same people, and doing the same job. It is up to him to find meaning in work that many regard as menial, as necessary and yet as undervalued as prayer.

As we mature, accepting more responsibility for our lives means finding work that will enable us to support ourselves. It's often a rite of passage from childhood dreams to an adult understanding of our true strengths and limitations. The fifteen-year-old Elton John wannabe may find himself at thirty working in a store that sells musical instruments. The eighteen-year-old determined to write the next Great American Novel may decide it makes more sense to become a librarian than try to write full-time. And both may discover that they love their jobs.

Breakthroughs happen. The American poet May Swenson made a good living as an executive secretary on Wall Street before winning the Pulitzer Prize for Poetry. Many of her work colleagues had not known she was a writer. Her job had provided enough money for her basic survival, and she was dedicated and disciplined enough to continue to pursue her vocation, even when no one was paying attention.

Paterson writes poetry but isn't seeking attention for that—or anything else. He's a humble man. It is the way he uses his time, and respects other people, that encourages me to believe that he is a true artist. He doesn't put on airs but takes his responsibilities as a bus driver seriously, arriving on time every morning to make sure his bus is in good condition. He notices his passengers and enjoys overhearing their conversations. One day when his bus breaks down, he is like a mother hen; his main concern is making sure that everyone is all right. He's made room to truly care about others and also nourish his deepest desire, which is to write.

Paterson's secret is that, like a monk, he has stripped his life down to essentials so that he can focus on what matters most. He doesn't have to decide what to eat for breakfast; it's always a bowl of cereal. This frees him to take out a little notebook as he eats and compose meditative poems about things as ordinary as matches and as profound as his love for his wife. He doesn't have to concern himself with what to do on his lunch break; every day he takes a sandwich to a park bench near a waterfall. All morning he's been working on verse in his head, allowing lines to appear, change, and disappear. Now he writes down what has come to him over the morning hours. Slowly—and the movie proceeds at a remarkably slow and deliberate pace—you come to realize that Paterson has used his daily schedule to build a glorious interior life.

Monastic people often speak of having a "vocation," of feeling that they have been called to monastic life. Most Americans would not consider bus driving a career, let alone a vocation. It's just a job that pays the bills, without much opportunity for advancement. But Paterson does have a vocation, as a poet. And that makes the film compelling.

A job will earn us a living, but it's often called the daily grind, something that wears us down. A vocation is something else entirely. The word is ancient, coming from Sanskrit and Latin, and at its root it means "voice." If you have a vocation, you have found your voice. We can easily feel trapped in the rut of routine, but both monks and Paterson know that routine can be a scaffold that supports a rich and rewarding life.

At home, Paterson has a small space in the basement full of books, including those by Paterson native William Carlos

Williams. He seems bemused when his wife, Laura, tells him that she wants to make copies of the poems in his notebook so that others can enjoy them, but typically, he agrees to let her do it.

Much in this film is left unexplained. It often points to flash points in American society but takes them in stride. We encounter the diversity of the American workplace, as the manager at the city bus terminal, a husband and father who feels overburdened and unloads his concerns on Paterson every morning, is an immigrant from India. We see a framed photograph of Paterson in his uniform as a United States Marine and learn that the wife he adores is of Middle Eastern descent. Played by Iranian actor Golshifteh Farahani, her endearingly enthusiastic following of whims leavens the film, and Paterson's life, with humor.

Paterson leaves us with questions about race and class in America. At the bar to which Paterson goes every night to nurse a single beer, he is the only white patron. But he's known there, just part of the neighborhood scene. His conversations with the bar owner, the great actor Barry Shabaka Henley, with his hangdog, seen-it-all face, are priceless. I would watch the film again just to catch more of the photos on the bar's back wall of famous Paterson natives, including Allen Ginsberg and Lou Costello. Our poet, a gentle and thoughtful man, was trained by the Marines to take quick and effective action to defuse potentially dangerous situations, a skill that comes in handy one night at the bar.

Paterson is so placid and given to routine that one might wonder if he suffers from the post-traumatic stress syndrome that afflicts many veterans who have endured the horrors of combat. For people with PTSD, any interruption in a carefully constructed routine can be disastrous. But Paterson handles disruptions well, as when his bus breaks down or when he must disarm a friend at the bar. And the man remains a friend. When Paterson arrives at the bar one night with the family dog in tow, some gangbangers in a car stop and ask him how much the dog is worth; they suggest he might be a target for dognapping. Many people would regard this as a threat: Paterson, true to form, engages the men in a brief but genial conversation before they drive off.

One scene from the film, in which a privileged and precocious preteen girl happens to meet Paterson and is astonished that a bus driver likes Emily Dickinson and writes poetry himself, strikes me as essential to understanding the depth of *Paterson*. So much of American society, from the places we live and work to where we socialize, is divided by class, and I like to imagine that meeting Paterson has given this girl something to ponder. I had the great advantage of living for twenty-five years in a small South Dakota town where my neighbors included a city police officer, a rancher and farmer, and a driver of long-haul semitrucks. I quickly learned that intelligence knows no class and that I would rather spend time with the waitress who discovered *Anna Karenina* in the library where I worked and loved it, instead of the English teacher, a recent graduate of a teachers college, who had never read a novel by Charles Dickens and had no interest in starting now.

I try not to assume that when I meet someone in a service job they don't have something to teach me. When I learned that a taxi driver in Chicago was from Nigeria and told him that I loved the writing of Wole Soyinka, he said, proudly, "He is my tribesman," and I learned a little about what it meant to him to be Yoruba. And I had a remarkable conversation with a man who was driving a cab in St. Louis. In heavily accented English he startled me by asking unexpectedly what I thought of Mark Twain. My response allowed him to tell me that he'd taught literature in Russia before immigrating to America, and when I told him that I love *The Master and Margarita*, Mikhail Bulgakov's daring satire of Stalin's regime, he replied that the author had included many features—puns and clicking sounds—that can be appreciated only if you know Russian. He recited a long passage from the novel to prove his point.

The quiet radicalism of *Paterson* lies in its trusting us to recognize that its bus driver, a seemingly ordinary working-class guy, is a man worthy of our attention. It is radical also in its engagement with the simple flow of life, without fanfare, contrivance, or manipulation. Once when I watched it with friends, a woman commented, "I liked it, but I kept waiting for something to happen." A Buddhist monk who was present replied, "Are you kidding? It happens every day!" There isn't much plot to discuss, although near the film's end the little dog that Paterson tolerates for the sake of his wife creates a sad and painful situation for him.

I first saw *Paterson* on an airplane, and as the film ended a flight attendant asked me if I was okay, as I was weeping. "Oh, thank you," I replied. "I'm fine. I've been watching a beautiful film, and the ending caught me by surprise." I can safely say that *Paterson* is the only film whose conclusion brought not only tears but thoughts of the archangel Raphael. His name means "God's Healer," and Raphael is the angel charged with making sure that we meet all the people in our lives we are meant to encounter. Paterson has made a good life for himself and his wife, but when unexpected trouble comes and he needs healing, it comes from a most unlikely stranger.

Gareth

Paterson is about making paradise and beginning again every day, wherever you are. Its crazy-beautiful idea makes it honestly inspirational, close to holy. Inspirational because it takes an ordinary guy in an ordinary town and shows us how to see our own ordinariness as full of wonder; holy because this ordinary guy is an icon of integrity—he loves, he lets his yes be yes, and bigotry finds no foothold in him.

The crazy-beautiful idea is that everyone is an artist, and when not subjected to the trappings of materialism, creativity can just flow as part of everyday life. This does not mean, of course, that all of us should know what to do with a paintbrush and egg tempera or a pencil and iambic pentameter. We can, however, resist the coercions to prioritize making more money or having more things no matter what the cost and instead claim meaningful lives regardless of the attention or financial rewards.

Adam Driver is perfectly ordinary enough to be a gift in the lead role (Paterson his name, Paterson his town), gently containing his tall muscular frame but ready to use it to protect. The Iranian actor Golshifteh Farahani brings a lovely, mild eccentricity to the woman Paterson loves; their kindness and dreaming together make a modest house a palace.

Paterson unfolds over a week with the rhythm of poetry, and each day's experience reveals more about the people we're watching. *Paterson* has been called a "utopian" film, and it earns that term. For one thing, *Paterson*'s community is among the most racially diverse in movies—with distinct African American, Indian American, and Middle Eastern voices. The average white guy is the minority and is content. Not only is he not striving for the public acclaim typical of struggling artist stories; he is also so mindful about the world and his place in it that his writing is simply a manifestation of his life.

We may balk at the notion of someone so dedicated to poetry keeping his work in one notebook, uncopied. But there's a purity there that fits with the ego-free way he treats his art.

Just as the film is structured like a poem, the form and content of Paterson's life are in alignment too. Paterson's daily habits are, as Kathleen suggests, monk-like: sanding down to the grain of what matters. Disciplines of soul-craft may *look* rigid, but they are not a mental boot camp that makes us more android-like than soulful. Paterson does the same thing pretty much every day, but it's life-giving. One way to tell if a habit is soul-work or more like psychological industrialism, a conveyor belt to fake spiritual growth, is to ask if it brings more love into the world. If your standards and practices help you get that right, much else—maybe everything—will fall into place. And if you avoid a rhythm of life that honors what human beings actually are, then nothing else will work, even if everyone buys your books and you never need to ride the bus again.

Paterson may or may not be conscious of what's working in *his* life, but the fact that he bravely uses his skills to intervene in a potentially lethal incident, not only keeping everyone alive but remaining on good terms with the antagonist, is evidence that protective courage and love poetry belong together.

He may also not notice, nor does the film remark on, the most idyllic fact of his life: in an era where loud voices tell us to fear the other, home is a white US American veteran and a brown-skinned Middle Eastern free spirit, two artists reconciling their differences and figuring out life together. Another crazy-beautiful idea, but more beautiful than crazy.

One of my favorite moments in cinema has an elderly doctor and a thirty-five-year-old farmer in a late-night hushed conversation. The movie is *Field of Dreams*, which is far more thoughtful than its title. The doctor tells the farmer that a long time ago he had a brief opportunity to become a professional baseball player, only to have it snatched away by pure chance. The farmer responds, "It would *kill* some men to get so close to their dream and not touch it. God, they'd consider it a tragedy."

Doc Graham responds with words about vocation that I want to live by and that might help me make wherever I am, and whatever I'm doing, more like Paterson: "Son, if I'd only gotten to be a doctor for five minutes . . . now that would have been a tragedy."

Paterson's vocation is to live his life counter to the spirit of the age, which always wants more: more attention, more money, more things, more ease, more *me*. Paterson shows that if your desires are whole, you might actually be able to get everything you want. Once you figure out the difference between the soul of a vocation and its trappings, you can experience its magic even if it doesn't look exactly how you had imagined it on the outside. Paterson is not just a poet who drives a bus or a bus driver who writes poetry. He's both.

I once heard that Stephen King responds to people who ask him, "How can I become a writer?" with "Do you mean *How can I become someone who writes?* or do you mean *How can I become famous and do book tours?*" Of course, it's not bad to want others to read your work, but if you're not writing for the sake of writing, you may not actually be a writer.

For those of us who once dreamed of playing rock music in a stadium full of raving fans, may we come to know that it is not (necessarily) a limitation to work in a record store instead. That work—or the work of painting a small house, or baking cupcakes, or getting people from one place to another—can be invested with the magic of the calling beneath the surface. Being a rock star might be exciting for a while, but it often turns bitter. Especially if it divides you from your soul or stops you from appreciating the magnificence of a clutch of plums in the fridge.

Questions and Conversations

1. What dreams were you encouraged to have when you were younger?
2. What dreams would you have now if you were totally free to imagine your life meeting its purpose?
3. What everyday or "ordinary" things in your life do you enjoy the most? Does this tell you anything about what you're here for?
4. Do you think Paterson is a poet who drives a bus or a bus driver who writes poetry? Or is his vocation to be fully himself in both roles?
5. What would you like to do that helps you come alive, especially if this thing has become dormant in your life?

6

VOCATION—TO STEP INTO YOUR OWN SHOES

Malcolm X (USA, 1992)
Directed by Spike Lee, written by Spike Lee and Arnold Perl

One of the most comprehensive and politically resonant bi-opics, charting the spiritual development of one of the most important and misunderstood figures of the twentieth century.

Gareth

Malcolm X begins as angry sermon and ends as exhorta-tion, telling the story of a life more comprehensively, with more psychological nuance and spiritual credibility than any biopic should be expected to handle in three hours. It's an astonishing portrayal of a time and a person, an honoring of a life and vision, and a challenge.

The opening oration is stark, charging "the white man" with the monstrosity of anti-Black racism. "We're the living proof of those charges," says Denzel Washington (in the masterpiece of his craft) as Malcolm over footage of the 1991 police beating of Rodney King. It's an extraordinary beginning: big studio movies almost never start with an explicit political confrontation. Spike Lee neither dilutes Malcolm's life for the mainstream (mostly white) audience nor preaches to the choir. The opening announces that this film is for everyone. Who you believe yourself to be will determine whether you are mirrored or provoked.

If you feel seen, that's the point. If you're uncomfortable, that's the point too. *Malcolm X* reveals its protagonist as one who suffered beyond many imaginations, responded to trauma with rage and courage, and evolved into one of the most whole people, claiming equality, self-respect, and the dignity of *all* people, dying "unconquered still." This does not imply we must pretend he was perfect. Aside from being absurd, this is not a helpful way to think about someone we may wish to emulate. Three decades after the film's release, the historian Peniel E. Joseph wrote,

> The . . . notion of identity as a fixed . . . quality is undergoing a profound reconsideration. . . . We are . . . better equipped to appreciate Malcolm X's contradictions. . . . When we see Malcolm X's humanity in all its contingencies, complexities, and vulnerabilities, only then can we relate to, and be inspired by, Malcolm's story even when—especially when—he disappoints us. . . . Malcolm X is certainly a figure worthy of veneration. But we must never lose sight of the man.[1]

The life of Malcolm the man teaches that becoming our truest selves is inextricably linked to doing the most we can to build a safer, fairer, and more compassionate world.

▲▼▲

Malcolm X traces the spiritual development of a real person—his childhood, suffering, mistakes, maturing, and confrontation with the questions of responsibility and the soul. We see his courage, grappling with ideas, conversion, and being mentored and betrayed. We see the terrors to which he was subjected and how he tried to live in service to love. *Malcolm X* glimpses the soul of a man beloved and admired, misunderstood and denounced. It wants the best for the world, even for those in the world who don't. As Ossie Davis's eulogy has it, "[He] didn't hesitate to die, because he loved us so. When we honor him, we honor the best in ourselves." Taking Malcolm X seriously means taking ourselves seriously.

Biopics rarely achieve what *Malcolm X* does; it's about not only the protagonist but the world that shaped him and that he shaped in return. Malcolm X didn't come out of nowhere. The world existed before he did and presented him with gifts and challenges; the world exists now after he has left us, but it would not be the same world had he never been.

This is true for every human being. For some of us the capacity to choose how we will respond to circumstances may be the *only* thing we feel empowered to do; for all of us, it may be the most important.

We are born into contexts of complicity and burden, of privilege and gift. We have a responsibility to discern what we are here for. But before we can do that, we need to know who we are. And we cannot answer the question of who we are without learning *where* we are. The questions Malcolm faces are the same that you and I must face, albeit at a different scale: What are my needs and burdens, and how should I live with them? Who are the safer, wiser people and spaces to help release them, and what medicine do I carry that will help nudge the world around me into more wholeness?

These questions do not apply only to the "great people" of history or those who found large platforms from which to speak. Each of us is a universe, and so if we affect the life of only one other person, that's two universes—more than enough! And for that matter, public platforms come to people almost always as a matter of luck or tragedy, being the right (or wrong) person in the right (or wrong) place at the right (or wrong) time. A life's meaning is not best evaluated by how many heard your voice, read your books, or followed your lead. The only size that matters is the size of the openness of your heart to the inner call of where your gifts meet the needs of the world.

Saying this, I want to acknowledge that I am a white man reflecting on a film about a Black man who was subject to torments such that my social identity and privileges mean I may not even be able to *imagine* them. There are people who can more legitimately identify with Malcolm X, and there are those who would—consciously or otherwise—appropriate or exploit his memory. But there are no legitimate barriers to *seeking to learn* from the life of any other human. As Charles Eisenstein says, the best question we can be asking of each other is, "What is it like to be you?"[2]

Malcolm X is a vision of what it might have been like to be Malcolm at four distinct stages of his life. The golden light of Malcolm Little's early life crashing into the horror of his father's murder; the vibrancy of Detroit Red's young adulthood; the humor and the grace; the rapscallion nature and borderline menace of his criminal activities; the physical imprisonment leading to the acceleration of his journey toward freeing himself on the inside and becoming Malcolm X; the culmination and integration of the wound, the compassion, the charisma, the leadership, and the humanitarian vision embodied in Brother el-Hajj Malik el-Shabazz.

The movie begins with a litany of sorrow and torment mingling with boogie-woogie dancing and light (and fantastic costumes!). The Klan terrorizes Malcolm's family, riding off into an enormous moon, a moon larger than it ever actually looks but exactly the size it might appear in a child's traumatized memory. That scene, so early in the film, is so breathtaking, so horrifying, so cinematic: it seeks to erase D. W. Griffith's despicably racist and massively influential *The Birth of a Nation* (1915). That film is often justified due to its pioneering cinematic techniques, but *Malcolm X* shows that you can of course announce new cinematic techniques and serve the common good at the same time. This is a truly great movie. Like Andrei Tarkovsky's masterpiece, *Andrei Rublev*, it seems to touch on every available genre—from musical to horror, comedy to history. It's not just a story about the man himself but also a vision of what America has been, is, and could be.

Malcolm's conversion in prison feels like an invitation to an entire nation, and *Malcolm X* recognizes that conversion to a spiritual path is a lifelong process. It shouldn't surprise us that Malcolm's earlier views were more exclusionary: he had every reason to want to hold white people at bay, and it's typical of the first step after a religious conversion to be overzealous. Malcolm's Middle East journey deepened his experience of the unity of all people. In all traditions, it is the contemplatives and mystics who are always most open to the light in others, but this doesn't happen overnight.

▲▼▲

The shocking gunshot sound effect scattered throughout the movie telegraphs what Malcolm may always have known and perhaps helped him face his own death before it happened. These are mighty notions—life and death, the things we can and cannot control, the possibility of change. And this is where *Malcolm X* is most unusually helpful as a cinematic mentor. This man suffered intensely, and made mistakes, and mistreated people, and this man *changed*. He didn't amputate his various selves but sought to live into the best version of all the different Malcolms—not perfect, but willing to be perfected. (One of the most moving moments is one of the simplest, when Malcolm apologizes to a woman for being testy with her. Even amid the unbearable tension of knowing his life to be at imminent risk, he still surrenders to the movement of love and character.)

The magnificent Delroy Lindo, who plays West Indian Archie, has said this of Malcolm: "[He] was able to make a U-turn . . . and re-apply himself so fervently to this other endeavor. . . . If Malcolm Little can become Malcolm X, there is hope that . . . I can redeem my life."[3]

Vocation is often misunderstood as if there were a kind of predetermined metaphysical subway route. I think, rather, that vocation includes what we do, but *how* we do it matters more. The person I talk with most often, the writer and spiritual director Brian Ammons, says it all the time. Brian pierces the damaging assumption that vocation is a flowchart for the "what" of life rather than a deep calling to deep regarding a "way" of life, and he repudiates the notion that only "professionally holy people" have vocations rather than every human who bears the image of love whether they know it or not. Plenty of people are gifted with a compelling public speaking style but lack the heart of a servant leader; plenty misdirect their gift for organizing into the mere "making" of money; and plenty have been told that because their voices are quieter, and their enthusiasms less public, their lives matter less than the loudest ones. Many of us have been taught to confuse the substance of calling with its structure—such as when someone conflates a calling to pastoral ministry with being employed by a particular institution.

None of these are helpful or accurate ideas about vocation. A calling to serve the common good from the place where our compassion (which derives partly from our wounds) and our gifts meet is not the same thing as a GPS route, with every possible turn mapped out in advance. What we do and how we do it cannot be disentangled. Things change. Vocation properly understood and in the context of interdependent community and accountable mentorship does not remain static; it will transform us throughout life.

So when I watch *Malcolm X*, I think about how to take my life as seriously as he did. I think about the stages I have passed through and am holding loosely, and I anticipate (even more loosely) the stages to come. I consider my wounds and how they might be transformed beyond the myth of redemptive violence (the idea that we can bring order out of chaos through killing our "enemies") without falling into the myth of redemptive suffering (the idea that some people should unjustly bear the pain of the rest of us). I'm grateful to the extraordinary teacher Melvin Bray for introducing me to the concept of the myth of redemptive suffering and for encouraging me to take Malcolm X seriously. I reflect on my complicity in wounds caused to others; am I one of the "good white Christians [who] would not stand for his troublemaking"? I ask myself what it would mean to become the best version of myself. I ask who wants the best for me, like Betty Shabazz, who in Angela Bassett's indelible performance is the kind of queen who calls forth the regal-divine in her husband and in anyone who would witness their relationship.

Likely none of us will have a life as influential as Malcolm X. But I get the sense that he would challenge the comparison. What matters is not what you do compared to what he did but what you do compared to the resources, the learning, the mentoring, the needs in the world you inhabit. Malcolm X (and *Malcolm X*) envisages being most fully human as indivisible from self-giving action on behalf of the vulnerable. You cannot fully be a person without caring for the needs of others. You do not need to be famous or world-influencing to do that. Malcolm is, as the writer Barry Michael Cooper says, "calling us to live up to something,"[4] but that something is not to step into his shoes. It is to step into our own.

Kathleen

Spike Lee's brilliant and challenging *Malcolm X* brings Psalm 137 to mind. It is a psalm of exile, a lament written after the people of ancient Israel had been forcibly taken from their homes in Jerusalem and enslaved in far-off Babylon. The psalmist writes that a new and terrible demand is being made of them, "For it was there that they asked us, our captors, for songs, our oppressors, for joy" (v. 3).[5] The Babylonians regarded these slaves and their culture as exotic and their traditional songs as good entertainment.

When Psalm 137 is used in Christian worship, its ending verses are usually omitted. They read, "O Babylon, destroyer, they are happy who repay you the ills you brought on us. They shall seize and shall dash your children on the rock!" (vv. 8–9).[6] I find this a useful passage for spiritual reflection. It does not endorse the murder of innocent children but acknowledges it as a horror that the Israelites had witnessed happening to their own children, and it also compels me to admit that such atrocities happen in our world today.

The wish for one's enemies to be repaid in the most brutal way for the evils they have committed is exactly what you might expect from a people who have been exiled, abused, and enslaved. And when I consider Malcolm X's hard-to-hear words about all white people being devils and irredeemably evil, Psalm 137 makes me reflect: of course. When the Ku Klux Klan has murdered your father and burned your house down, you can feel that you have seen the devil. When you have been continually disrespected and demeaned by white bosses, it is easy to generalize about the race of those abusing you.

We must never mistake the angry words the younger Malcolm uses to describe white people with the "hate speech" we so often hear today. He is addressing actual injustices inflicted on Black people in America throughout its history, not, as so many politicians do today, inventing an "other" onto which they project their fears. One danger for us is that their fearmongering for political advantage has desensitized us to despicable language and made it more difficult for us to discern the truth in what Malcolm X is trying to tell us, truths we need to hear.

But if the negative language in *Malcolm X* begins to get you down, it might help to recognize that there is not a single emotion expressed in the film that you can't find in the Psalms.

The willingness of Malcolm X to change and grow is inspiring: he became someone who could say, after his conversion to Sunni Islam and a pilgrimage to Mecca, "I've had enough of someone else's propaganda. . . . I'm for truth, no matter who tells it. I'm for justice, no matter who it is for or against. I'm a human being first and foremost, and as such I'm for whoever and whatever benefits humanity as a whole."[7] While he had once condemned all whites, he pledges to never "be guilty of that again. . . . The true Islam has shown me that a blanket indictment of all white people is as wrong as when whites make blanket indictments against Blacks."[8]

Those words, wrested from hard experience and fostered by a remarkable willingness to grow as a person, come from *The Autobiography of Malcolm X*. Its subtitle is "As Told to Alex Haley," but the voice of its subject comes through loud and clear, and I'd recommend the book as an adjunct to viewing Spike Lee's film. Growing up in Hawaii (a place that reflects the world as it is, mostly Asian), I'd read about the civil rights struggles on the US mainland, but they felt remote from me. I was horrified by photographs of "Whites Only" signs on restrooms and admired the work of people like Martin Luther King Jr. But I knew Malcolm X only as a firebrand speaker denouncing whites. He himself had predicted that most Americans would see him this way, saying to Haley, "When I am dead . . . the white man, in his press, is going to identify me with 'hate.' He will make use of me dead, as he has made use of me alive, as a convenient symbol, of 'hatred.'" But Malcolm X insists that "all I have been doing is holding up a mirror to reflect, to show, the history of unspeakable crimes that his race has committed against my race."[9]

I am indebted to a mentor who recommended that I read *The Autobiography of Malcolm X* in the early 1970s when I was in my early twenties. In the book I encountered a man who, though he was clearly bright, had been discouraged by his teachers from pursuing anything other than vocational education. (A chilling scene depicts that in the film.) It was no surprise that he had chosen the life of a street hustler and petty criminal rather than accept low-wage work. But I was amazed to find that when he was in prison and realized how limited his vocabulary was, he decided to change that by reading and studying the dictionary.

I still encounter people who resist the term *systemic racism*, but it's been part of America since the founding of the nation, when the authors of the Constitution designated enslaved Black people as three-fifths of a human being. And in 1944, when the GI Bill boosted many American veterans into the middle class, Southern senators made sure that the bill accommodated Jim Crow laws so that Black veterans would not be eligible for its benefits. It was not until 2021 that the US Congress looked at remedying that.

I love so much of what Gareth has written about this film: noting that the impossibly enormous moon that appears on the night when young Malcolm Little's family is being terrorized by the Klan is exactly what a frightened child would see. And I'm grateful for his calling out the hideous racist excesses of D. W. Griffith's *The Birth of a Nation*, which presents Blacks—especially Black men—as subhuman predators. That unfortunately influential film spurred the growth of the Klan in America throughout the 1920s and no doubt emboldened Klan members to target and murder men like Malcolm Little's father, an outspoken Baptist preacher. Spike Lee's ambitious *Malcolm X* is, as Roger Ebert has stated, "one of the great screen biographies," as it does a fine job of presenting a complex man in full but also presents a broad commentary on America in the twentieth century.[10]

I agree with Gareth that the way for viewers to appreciate *Malcolm X* is not to distance ourselves from a man we may think of as controversial or unworthy of consideration. Lee's film makes it clear that the spiritual journey of Malcolm X is one that we all undertake. Who are we? What are we meant to do with our talents, gifts, and privileges? How do we face the obstacles others put in our way? How can we live so as to benefit our community and the human race?

Questions and Conversations

1. What have you believed about vocation—where it comes from, what it's for, how it works?
2. What do you think your vocation is—in other words, what kind of world would you like to see, and what role can you play in that?
3. Knowing more about *what* you feel called to, discuss *how* you feel called to do it.
4. What pilgrimage might you need to take—an external one (like Malcolm takes to Mecca), an inner journey, or both?
5. Reflecting on the moment when Malcolm apologizes for being disrespectful and raising his voice, consider parts of how you show up in the world that you would like to change.
6. Where does your life intersect with that of Malcolm X—either as someone who feels seen by his story or provoked by it?

7

RELATIONSHIPS

Make Way for Tomorrow (USA, 1937)

Directed by Leo McCarey, written by Viña Delmar

Barkley and Lucy Cooper (Victor Moore and Beulah Bondi) have their home taken from them by the bank due to ageism, fear of asking for help, and the individualism of a new generation.

Love Is Strange (USA, 2014)

Directed and written by Ira Sachs

Ben Hull and George Garea (John Lithgow and Alfred Molina) have their home taken from them, effectively by the church, due to homophobia, fear of asking for what they deserve, and the individualism of a new generation.

Gareth

Love *is* strange—perhaps the thing that most affects us but that we least understand. It shows up in a vast range of our popular culture and most meaningful exchanges (we say it conquers all and that we can't live without it), but we rarely define love beyond vague sentimentality. Or worse, when we say *we love someone* what we really mean is *we love what they do for us*, or that we need them. How strange that we can't thrive without love—indeed, the path to a whole life *depends* on love—but we might not be able to say what the word means.

Movies, like music and literature, not to mention religion and politics, have helped and hindered how we understand love, especially in the context of relationships between people (as opposed to the love a person can have for the ecosystem, a cause, or life itself). It would be obvious to explore the question of love through cinematic depictions of marriage and partnership, but it would also be limiting. Many permutations of meaningful relationship deserve attention in an exploration of cinema, spirituality, and the cycle of life, so while this chapter focuses on two films ostensibly about marriage, it aims to take friendship and community seriously too.

The meaning of marriage is changing (as it always has), many people aren't married, and of course there is so much more to relationships than marriage. Yet movies about love usually focus on the courtship of two people, sometimes featuring conversations with their friends, perhaps with a culminating wedding scene. They typically don't tell us much about the complexity of love—to begin with, the way that love is at least as much about how we serve each other's well-being, not just how someone else makes us feel. Such movies often hermetically seal the protagonists, relegating others to window dressing. This isn't realistic; even for those of us who are in the happiest of marriages or partnerships, there is far more to life than that principal relationship; and of course, you don't have to be partnered to have profoundly meaningful connections with others.

Some of the best films about marriage are actually about divorce, and they serve as reminders of the tenderness required when two people who once found their home in each other later discover that it has an irreparable fault line beneath it.

And good films about friendship help us see what the most integrated friendship always does: reflects the light and shadow within us, points the way to alignment with our truest selves, and shows us that we don't have to be alone.

Then there are stories about "chosen family." I'm thinking of relationships involving more than two people not partnered to each other, in which a deeper experience is occurring about our callings, gifts, and needs; where people know they are safe, or at least safe enough, to be themselves; and when things go wrong there is a place the community members can fall without harming themselves.

As with all stories, what sometimes matters most is not so much what happens but what doesn't. Seeing a codependent relationship portrayed can heighten our awareness of what an interdependent one could look like; seeing loneliness calls forth hospitality; seeing people dancing on the edges of what's real but never quite getting to the heart of the matter can leave us more committed to making our communities more authentic.

Two films that consider all kinds of relationship, despite on the face of them being about marriage, are *Make Way for Tomorrow* and *Love Is Strange*, made over seventy-five years apart (one is a definite homage to the other). Each is about a couple forced to part because of the selfishness or lack of awareness in their circle. Each is also about the friendship between the couple and among others, the impact of the marriage on the community, and the community's relationship with the marriage.

Many traditions invite the wider chosen family to support people getting married. "In sickness and in health" is supposed to be a community effort, although we may rarely see such commitments embodied. Poetic words may be ritually spoken, but the aspirations behind these words often remain merely wishes.

In *Make Way for Tomorrow*, which Orson Welles called "the saddest movie ever made,"[1] Barkley and Lucy represent the first generation of people in the industrial age whose children don't see it as their duty to care for their parents. The emerging nuclear family colliding with the end of interdependent villages, the thirst for city life, the magic of a memorable day in which the tenderness between two people represents a lifetime's relationship—this film is handling a lot.

And *Love Is Strange* lets us see Ben and George's wedding, the role they play in their community, and how homophobia and other structural nightmares add unnecessary burdens and give other people the excuse to pretend they aren't their brothers' keeper. It's a more sophisticated film than *Make Way for Tomorrow* because it lets us see into the lives of their extended family. We see Kate (Marisa Tomei) and Elliot (Darren Burrows) dealing with how a yearning for purpose often collides with egotism and competition between partners and how parenting is frequently a stumble in the dark. The most hopeful element of *Love Is Strange* is how it points to a new generation nurtured in the embrace of multiple interdependent and open-minded connections, with an understanding of community that transcends the independent nuclear household economy.

As I said, what's strangest about love is that for something considered to be universally important and that should be prioritized over everything else (not just in the teaching that says "Love God and love your neighbor as yourself" or all the other synonyms for the Golden Rule), it's almost never defined in public. We find it easier to talk about taxes, war, and shiny objects worn by celebrities than about the thing we most want and need.

Love—the willingness to give yourself for the benefit of another—is *alive* between Barkley and Lucy, and between George and Ben. Their children, both literal and figurative, don't love Barkley, Lucy, George, and Ben that way, probably because they don't love *themselves* that way yet. But it may be that witnessing this kind of love, even when the people involved in it must part through cruel circumstance, helps others grow. I sometimes wince when I think of how as a child I might have hurt my parents through a lack of gratitude. Of course it's unreasonable to expect a child to know that, and part of the reason we have such experiences is so that later when other people are absent or ignorant, we get to pay the patience forward. We often learn love in the light of seeing it expressed to us when we needed it, even if we couldn't honor it; sometimes the learning comes a long time after the teaching.

Ben, George, Lucy, and Barkley don't dwell on the self-centeredness of the people in their lives whom they could have reasonably expected to take care of them. That's partly a function of their own kindness, but it's also a problem. Barkley and Lucy don't know how to ask for what they need, never mind what they want. What their culture calls "good manners" (but is actually emotional stuntedness resulting from social repression) mingles with rugged individualism to produce a lie that sounds gentle but is utterly toxic: *people should be able to take care of themselves, so let's not bother anyone else with our problems.*

Ben and George do ask for what they need, to begin with, and they have a deeper community network. But what oppresses them is not just the cruelty of the church firing George, or the relative uselessness of the well-intended but hopelessly inadequate city-subsidized housing program, but also the internalized homophobia that leads them to believe (or at least act as if) they are not worthy of the support.

If George and Ben were to believe "We have served this community for decades, and we are suffering because of dehumanizing prejudice and a refusal to take seriously contemporary wisdom in favor of willfully misreading a two-thousand-year-old book—all we are asking is that we not be separated," what sane person could disagree? They shouldn't have to say it, of course. Their allies should be ready to jump in.

And if Barkley and Lucy were to say, "We raised you—we gave you more than we had for ourselves, and we came of age at a time when elders had a reason to expect to be cared for by their children. We haven't asked for much, and we're nervous to do it now, but today we really are saying: please look up from your lives—all we're asking is that we not be separated," what sane person could disagree?

△▽△

Marriage and partnership can be insular or selfish, as with deep friendships and community. Marriage and partnership can carry an air of superiority, as if it is the best or most important form of relationship. But partnerships, friendships, and communities committed to learning love and wisdom can show the world how to live together.

As the relationship teacher David Schnarch brought to the fore, people can learn how to differentiate from others, to regulate our own anxiety, to know ourselves, to be non-reactive, and to tolerate discomfort for the sake of growth. Schnarch called this the "crucible approach," because close relationships are where the work of becoming human is most intense.[2] Learning the tools of the crucible deserves sustained attention throughout our lives; I don't know why we don't teach it in schools. Actually I do know: because our culture doesn't know how to love itself, never mind teach about love. Superficial songs and movies fake love, and political figures usually think it's a losing game to talk about love at all. But a serious engagement with love is a fundamental part of the kind of politics that the world actually needs.

If fascism is the belief that some lives are worth more than others, at the expense of everyone else's life, then the antidote is acting on the belief that everyone is equally worthy of love. Such a belief calls forth the mutual service of an ever-expanding loving relationship with all things, in which we would learn to stretch ourselves to serve one another's needs, without denying our own, so that everyone can flourish. Our posture toward one another would be nothing less than asking of everyone we meet, "How can I help make their life more whole?"

Such deep relationship takes more than two people. Those of us who are partnered had lives before we met the person with whom we are now sharing ours, and when one of us dies, the other will go on to more life without them. It's insane to expect marriage and partnership to survive without wider community. And it's not just offensive but painful to tell people who are not partnered that their relationships don't matter as much as the ones that include vows and parties and anniversaries.

Covenantal and sacred friendship matters just as much as marriage and often outlasts it. Even the people in a marriage might find that the sacred friendship between them is the most enduring part of the relationship.

▲▼▲

A story is told of an anthropologist studying a hunter-gatherer community and witnessing the major annual hunt. Seeing the community's leader parcel out meat for the whole village, she was perturbed—he had caught most of it, so why not keep it for himself?

The answer to the anthropologist is an answer to why Barkley and Lucy's children, and George and Ben's chosen family, should have gone the extra mile: "I store my meat in the belly of my friends."

When we believe the story that human beings are merely private individual economic units, more or less productive, responsible only—and entirely—for ourselves, we act more like robots, hoarders, or sentries. That individualistic story is a lie. What we really are is a dysfunctional but repairable family of interdependent beings, sacred and beautiful, called to love and serve from the resources we hold and to ask for help in the places we experience lack. We get to discern the safer people to ask for help and where to offer our gifts. Authentic relationship should help us transcend the shame of asking for what we need. Sometimes an urgent reality— like someone losing their home because of other people's selfishness—creates the circumstances where we get to help save someone's life. Sometimes it's *we* who are vulnerable, and the only way for our lives to be saved is to let others do the saving. We'll learn more about ourselves through participating in the messy, confusing, envelope-pushing, boundary-learning crucible of relationship than we ever can on our own.

Relationship is a huge risk—of being rejected, judged, misunderstood, and ultimately of experiencing the loss of the lover or the friend.

But the experience of being reflected back by another who knows us well, whether they are spouse, partner, friend, or community, may be the greatest location for spiritual growth.

We need living monuments to such relationship.

We need to study them.

We need to imagine what it would be like to join them.

And someone always needs to go first.

Kathleen

I'm glad Gareth noted that one of the strangest things about love is the difficulty we have in defining it. It may be our deepest need, but when it comes to love we expect our words to cover too wide a ground. We see the adolescent in the throes of a crush that mainly reveals that they're in love with love (I gasp in writing this, recalling my own youthful follies in this regard). We see that the sentimental love that initially makes a romance feel exciting tends to wither in the demands of the day-to-day, plunging us into heated arguments over whose turn it is to take out the garbage. And if we are fortunate, we've known the heartfelt, unconditional love of a parent and recognize that their example has allowed us to find ways to pass that love on to others.

Films can be invaluable in teaching us what love means in the context of our lives. Two films about divorce, *Kramer vs. Kramer* and *Marriage Story*, serve us admirably in revealing people who set aside their conflicts as they come to understand what it means to genuinely love their children. I found the ending of *Marriage Story* especially inspiring. It was sad to see that two people who had once loved each other could no longer stay married. But the love they had for their young son had transformed both parents into people who realized that their main priority was caring for him, and this set them free from the selfish concerns that had preoccupied them in a bitter divorce battle.

Films are so brief that they sometimes struggle to convey what a lifetime commitment to another person can mean. Both *Make Way for Tomorrow* and *Love Is Strange* are welcome exceptions. In one we have an elderly couple, Bark and Lucy, who have raised five children in the fifty years they've been married and are still very much in love. The other film gives us a middle-aged, childless gay couple, Ben and George. They've become devoted to each other over a forty-year relationship but have had to wait for laws to change to allow them to wed.

My parents were married for sixty-four years, and I've helped many Benedictine friends celebrate the fifty-year or sixty-year anniversary of their monastic vows. In all that time these people had to contend with a daunting amount of pain and trouble, struggling as fragile, vulnerable human beings to honor the commitments they had made when they were too young to fully understand what they were taking on.

But eventually the value and even the glory of their persistence had made itself known. I would even say that it had become visible in their faces, in their way of speaking and walking. Growing old together as a couple, or as an individual vowed to remain for life in a monastic community, they had found the "solace in love" that the apostle Paul speaks of in his letter to the early Christians of Philippi. The key, as

Paul notes, is learning to "do nothing from selfish ambition or empty conceit, but in humility regard others as better than yourselves. Let each of you look not to your own interests but to the interests of others" (Phil. 2:3–4).

We speak of "falling" in love but of "making" friendships. And I don't believe I have ever witnessed a long-term relationship in which the initial experience of love didn't evolve into a friendship by deliberate acts of self-sacrifice, choices made that allowed the relationship to continue and flourish. But this kind of maturity in love is remarkably difficult to achieve in a culture in which we are encouraged to resist deep commitments and keep our options open to take advantage of the next best thing. All that Paul recommends for enduring relationships is exactly what our society rejects.

The tragedy in both *Make Way for Tomorrow* and *Love Is Strange* initially comes from the outside: a bank foreclosing on a mortgage, church officials intolerant of a same-sex couple's marriage. But the sadness is compounded from within, by dysfunction and lack of empathy within the family. In both films the relatives don't truly see the couple or understand what it will mean for them to be separated. One wants to scream at the uncomprehending relatives and friends: "Pool your resources and find a place where this couple can live together; can't you see that they will not survive a separation?" The last image of *Make Way for Tomorrow* is haunting: we know Lucy to be a strong woman, but as she stands alone on a train platform, her face reflects utter disorientation at the departure of her beloved Bark.

The director of this film, Leo McCarey, made some of Hollywood's finest comedies, working with Mae West, W. C. Fields, the Marx Brothers, and Laurel and Hardy. And he allows humorous elements to emerge in this more serious film, as some of the couple's children are portrayed as comically clueless, shallow, and miserly. But one strength of both films is that the directors ask us not to judge these people. Especially in *Love Is Strange*, except for the narcissistic niece who is absorbed in New Age therapies for her imagined issues, we can probably relate to people who want to help their displaced relatives but are overcome with the pressures of parenting a teenager and trying to make a living, especially in the difficult fields of writing and entertainment. Good angels appear in both films, strangers who help the couples in unexpected ways, but they can't make up for family members who are unwilling or unable to offer adequate care. They also demonstrate that it is often easier to offer care to strangers than to relatives who can make legitimate, long-term claims on your time and attention.

Both films raise fundamental questions about how families and society care for people when the going gets rough, and that makes them contemporary to the core.

Make Way for Tomorrow was released in 1937, two years after the Social Security Act had passed Congress and before the act had been implemented and payments began to go to the elderly. Darryl Zanuck, the film's producer, wanted Mc-Carey to provide a happy ending, and while the film garnered praise from major directors such as John Ford and Frank Capra, Zanuck was correct in sensing that the film would not do well with people mired in an economic depression. They preferred to be entertained by cheery musicals, Shirley Temple, and Mickey Mouse. Even today a film depicting people in their seventies who are deeply in love would be a hard sell to studio executives and the public. But hey, let's loosen up, and revisit *Make Way for Tomorrow* and *Love Is Strange*, humming a chorus of "Let Me Call You Sweetheart" or "Baby You've Got What It Takes" as we go. Let's value Bark and Lucy and Ben and George for the old lovers they are, and picture them dancing happily into the past and even the future.

<hr>

Questions and Conversations

1. What are the most life-giving relationships you have known?
2. What do you believe about what makes marriage or partnership thrive?
3. Describe the best friendship you've had—what was it like, and what are some of the things you learned from it?
4. What has been the most important factor in sustaining the long relationships in your life, in friendships, marriage, or with family members?
5. What are the ingredients of an interdependent community, and have you experienced such a community in your life?
6. How do you contemplate your life and that of your significant other(s) or closest friends changing as you grow older? Where will your support come from?
7. Outside of your immediate family, what ties do you have with a broader community? How does that community affirm and sustain you?

$\mathcal{8}$

OVERCOMING SUCCESS

Faces Places (France, 2017)

Directed and written by Agnès Varda and J. R.

Faces Places is a road trip movie like none other, in which a renowned elderly filmmaker travels through France with a photographer in his thirties, engaging with people in small towns, farms, and factories. It expresses the highest purpose of art, which is to help us see others and ourselves with new eyes.

Kathleen

We live in a celebrity culture, and the entertainment business thrives by assessing some actors as "bankable," those who are likely to bring in tons of money, while writing off others as too unattractive or too old to succeed. How refreshing to find that Agnès Varda, one of France's national treasures, is not troubled that none of her films did well at the box office. "I don't relate to success," she has said. "I relate to making films."[1] And making films is what she did: beginning when she was twenty-five years old and ending not long before her death at ninety-one, she directed sixty-two of them.

Varda is an inspiration to any of us, demonstrating that true success means following our deepest desires, even if it means taking risks and ignoring social norms. She once explained in an interview that in the 1950s to become a film director in France, you first had to work as an apprentice, then as a third assistant director, then a second assistant director, then a first assistant director, and finally, when you were in your forties, you could direct. In 1955, with a background as a photographer and no experience in filmmaking, Varda and a small crew shot her first movie, *La Pointe Courte*.

The film is set in a fishing village in the South of France where Varda had lived as a child during World War II, and she proudly states that it contains "no dramatic events." Instead, like much of her work, it presents ordinary people in ordinary situations and includes both nonactors and professionals in its cast. The film exemplifies a principle that guided Varda over the years as she filmed neighbors working as bakers, butchers, and grocers: "Nothing is banal if you film people with empathy and love."

Varda and her husband, film director Jacques Demy, were precursors of the French New Wave in cinema that emerged in the 1950s. Directors including Jean-Luc Godard, François Truffaut, and Claude Chabrol defied conventional filmmaking in favor of experimenting with narrative and tackling major political and social issues. Within this movement Varda went her own way, focusing on women's issues and making documentaries about people on the outskirts of society.

Even Hollywood failed to seduce her. In the mid-1960s, following the success of her husband's film *The Umbrellas of Cherbourg*, a major studio invited him to Los Angeles to discuss a potential movie project. Varda says, "I followed like a good little wife, but I said if I don't like America, I'm going back." But she loved California, and while she was there, firmly believing, as she has said, that "chance has always been my best assistant," she tracked down a rumor of a possible relative, an artist in Sausalito. When she went to meet him, she found that he was her father's cousin, Jean, living on a houseboat that, given Varda's passion for bright colors, could have been a prop in one of her movies. She quickly decided to film their encounter and after a day and a half had a sweet eighteen-minute short, *Uncle Yanko* (1968).

Varda has said that three words have been essential in making her art: *inspiration*, *creativity*, and *sharing*. These strike me as important for any human endeavor: parenting, teaching, living a meaningful life. Varda had always centered her photographs and films on other people, but in 2000, when she was seventy-two, she found that newly available handheld digital cameras greatly enhanced her ability to approach others in a nonintimidating way. *The Gleaners and I* (2000) is one compelling result: initially inspired by Varda's observing people scavenging leftovers as an outdoor market closed, the film became a meditation on a centuries-old tradition in France.

The Widows of Noirmoutier (2006), which to my mind is Varda's most moving film, takes place in a small Breton fishing village. In a little over an hour, several women tell you everything about what it means to be a widow. Some were married for over fifty years, others for a few months. As they show faded wedding photographs and talk about their husbands' last days or the circumstances of their deaths and how they have coped with the devastating absence, it all rings true. When she made the film, Varda had been a widow for sixteen years, and you sense that these women are not only trusting her with their stories but confiding much that they have not admitted to anyone before.

Inspiration, creativity, and sharing are much in evidence in the delightful *Faces Places* (2017), as is Varda's daring nature. Few eighty-eight-year-olds would go on a road trip with a thirty-three-year-old in a hipster hat and shades in order to make a film. Few directors of any age would insist on funding the film with crowdsourcing to have complete freedom over its content.

But the photographer J. R. and Varda admired each other's work and decided to work together on a project in which they would take what Varda calls his "magic truck," a mobile photography studio that creates larger-than-life images, to rural and industrial areas in France. They then photographed people who volunteered to have their images placed on walls in their towns or in the factories or farms where they work. In one town people provided old photographs of their fathers and grandfathers, miners who had worked at a long-closed mine. The film crew enlarged the photographs and pasted them on the brick walls of row houses that had housed the miners and their families. One woman gasps upon seeing a photograph of her grandfather covering the building where she still lives, the last resident on a block scheduled for demolition. "What can I say?" she murmurs as she begins to weep.

The tall, lanky J. R. and diminutive Varda make an odd couple. There is plenty of love but also some intergenerational banter: "You're playing the wise grandmother," J. R. says, and Varda replies, "And you play the spirited young man." Varda shows J. R. an old film clip to prove that she once got Jean-Luc Godard to remove his sunglasses for her, implying that he could do the same. "They're not friendly," she says. But we learn, when J. R. takes Varda to meet his one-hundred-year-old grandmother, that he is not the too-cool-for-school guy he appears to be. He and his grandmother share a warm affection—her nickname for him is "Little Sweetie"—and we sense that his understanding of the aged runs deep. When he asks Varda if she's afraid of death, she replies that she thinks about it a lot, but adds, "I'm looking forward to it, because that'll be that."

Varda's increasingly blurred vision requires medical intervention. But she and J. R. play with it in a humorous way. They have people sit on tiers and hold up letters like the ones used in a vision test. People with the largest letters sit on the top row, and the letters dwindle in size with each row down. Varda likes the display but asks J. R. to tell the people to jiggle the letters up and down, because that is closer to what she sees with impaired vision.

The film ends on a poignant note. If Varda's fame and success have made her more open to the world, they have caused her old friend Godard to withdraw. When she goes to his home for an arranged visit, she is shocked to find the door locked, with no message left for her. J. R. tries to comfort Varda when her disappointment causes her to talk, uncharacteristically, more about the past than the present. What J. R. does with his sunglasses then is cause for celebration.

Faces Places was nominated for an Academy Award for Best Documentary, making Varda the oldest person ever nominated for a competitive Oscar. In 2019, when she was ninety-one, Varda gave her last interview, saying, "I fought for radical cinema all my life."[2] We need such radical artists who are more interested in truth than in success. We need people like Varda in every human endeavor, who don't mistake the trappings of success for the real thing, who seek to touch other people on a deep level. Varda reminds me to keep a low profile, never to think of myself as a "famous author," and to be wary of anyone who applies that term to me. I believe Varda would agree that the artist is best served by not being the center of attention but the attentive observer in the corner, the person no one notices.

A reviewer in the *New York Times* called Varda's last film, *Varda by Agnes* (2019), a retrospective look at her career, "a final visit with an irreplaceable filmmaker" who somehow feels like everyone's friend.[3] That's a fitting description for a woman, a born humanist, who says that she made films in order to share them. I will revisit and savor Varda's films for the rest of my life.

Gareth

Throughout *Faces Places* we're provoked to ask, What do you want, and how will you ask for it?

I'm touched by the delightful friendship between the elder stateswoman of French cinema and an emerging artist who understands himself enough to recognize that there are both things he does not know and things he must do. One face after another, expanded massively on the walls of their houses or barns, reveals the mundane as spectacular, honoring human beings as just "a little lower than the angels."

J. R. and Varda say they are "paying homage to the ordinary on a large scale," and their tender friendship is part of this. Varda's awareness of her mortality and the desire to create "as many images as we can before it's too late" is moving, married to J. R.'s spontaneity and a commitment to have no itinerary.

Varda's experience of Jean-Luc Godard at the end of *Faces Places* isn't just about her relationship with a notoriously difficult man or the history of cinema. Even if we have never seen their films, pretty much anyone alive today who is influenced by European culture has been touched by Varda and Godard, so it's about two people who shaped our experience of ourselves. It's also about archetypal regret for the past.

If we haven't already identified with the faces and places that have appeared prior to this awful moment of abandonment, Varda's grief at Godard's rejection calls us in. We know this feeling. But J. R.'s sunglasses are authentically rose-colored—the color of cheeks when tears fall, even tears of joy. We know this feeling too. You can't go home again, but if you learn to dance with other people's imperfections, you can make a new home with the people who will love you now.

We can imagine what Varda and Godard's reunion, titans of cinema and intimate friends, could have been. But this is far more about what life is really like—the ebb and flow of relationships creaking and challenging, living and dying. But it's Godard's tragedy, not Varda's. She knows that a self-image constructed by either the superficial acclaim of a crowd or an ideologically driven outsized notion of one's own importance isn't success at all. The measure of who you are has to do with the size of your heart.

It's an extravagant act of generosity for Agnès Varda to share this window into her own vulnerability and not to wrap things up with simple catharsis. The sad-happy story ends with a delicious joke that invites us to remember that you never know when a story is over, especially when you're in it; we are invited—literally—to see the world through Varda's eyes, and it validates our own dreams.

This is a movie about what really matters—not "winning" but becoming ourselves. It urges me to ask myself, What is the central story of me? From what vantage point do I read my own life? Do I truly recognize that your life has the same value to you as mine does to me?

And I am so attracted to Varda's deceptive lack of sophistication, which in her films is an invitation to something profound: If most of life is constituted by an encounter with faces, places, and stories, shouldn't I slow down enough to actually experience them?

Questions and Conversations

1. What do the words *inspiration*, *creativity*, and *sharing* signify to you? Maybe take each word individually and discuss how it applies to your everyday life.

2. What were you doing at the age of twenty-five? Can you imagine still being engaged in that activity when you're in your eighties or nineties?

3. What did success mean to you in the past, and what does it mean now? (Or what would you like it to mean?)

4. What does "doing things on your own terms" mean to you? Is it possible to include other people in that? If so, how?

5. What do you make of Varda's assertion that "nothing is banal if you film people with empathy and love"? Most of us aren't filmmakers—but does this perspective hold true in your life and work?

6. What are the best elements of the story you would like to tell about your life?

7. What is one step you could take, in the next week, to step into more of the elderhood you yearn for, to step into more of the kind of intergenerational friendship embodied in *Faces Places*, or to reimagine the story you're telling about yourself?

9

GENEROSITY

Babette's Feast (Denmark, 1987)

Directed and written by Gabriel Axel, from the story by Isak
Dinesen (Karen Blixen)

In 1871, an outsider on the verge of collapse is taken in by
the unemotive inhabitants of a remote Danish island. Over
time, she brings gifts of grace, especially in the form of a
meal that might forever change the lives of everyone on the
island.

Gareth

One Christmas Day, it was cold and rainy, and my heart was
broken. A loving relationship had fallen apart the previous
week, and I had stumbled through one sluggish day after
another. Friends had offered direct support on each of those
days, but I was in the kind of depressed fog that notices help
only retrospectively. But even my self-pity couldn't deny what
my friend Kyle did for me that night.

By the time I made it to Kyle's around 8:30 p.m., I hadn't eaten all day. We were meeting up to travel together to see our friends Caroline and Charmaine, brilliant sisters who hosted an annual gathering for people who by 9 p.m. on Christmas Day may want to be somewhere other than under their parents' roof. I loved that convening of waifs and strays—thirty and sometimes forty of us squeezed into a shoebox living room made for about eight, smoked salmon and wine on the table at 9:30 p.m.—the moment on Christmas Day when even those most satiated on the feast earlier that day discover a hitherto untapped second stomach. Kyle intuited that despite the fact of this much-anticipated smorgasbord only an hour away, I was hungry right now, and sad, and he could do something about it.

Retrieving Chinese takeout food from the fridge, he reheated some fried rice and lemon chicken. It overflowed a small plate, which is a lovely analogy for how boundaries can call forth happiness. There is an old joke about a grouch judging a restaurant's bad food as even worse due to the small portions; in reverse, the joke becomes a recipe for satisfaction: if you don't have much to give a friend, but it fills their plate, it might be even more than they need.

That night I ate like a prince, sitting on a torn old leather armchair by the fire. I was experiencing waves of love from Kyle, who may have had his own reasons to feel sad that Christmas but was giving his heart to help heal mine.

Which brings me to *Babette's Feast*, a film about a religious sect that has lost the meaning of the words it has turned into idols. The members of the sect live on a cold, isolated island, where the weather never seems to stray beyond different shades of cold, damp, and gray. Their regular meetings are facilitated by two women, daughters of the now deceased pastor, who was "greatly respected and perhaps a little feared." His followers meet to honor their founder, even though he has long since gone. Members of the sect greet each other with words like "Mercy and truth are met together; righteousness and delight shall kiss each other," without ever experiencing their meaning. A soldier visits the island and tells the daughters of how "piety was fashionable at court"; legalism happens in royal palaces too. But into their midst comes an outsider—Babette (played with fierce grace by Stéphane Audran), who has fled from France with nothing but her memories and culinary skill. Having lost everything, she is broken and alone. The daughters take her in, revealing that this community has warm principles, despite its cold demeanor.

Babette stays with them for over a decade, helping around the house, providing the Dickensian gruel that they seem content to eat; then, one day, a letter arrives. She has won the lottery, and the daughters are heartbroken because they assume this means she will leave them to return to her true home. Instead, she asks to cook a meal for the sisters and the sect. As the preparations for the meal develop, the sect members suspect the worst: the food seems dangerously worldly.

The sect members fear that "the world, the flesh, and the devil" have intruded on their lives. When the meal finally happens, they have agreed to stiffen resolve: to sit upright, not to have eye contact with the food, and, at all costs, *not to enjoy a single bite*. But, as they say, what happens next will amaze you. . . .

▲▼▲

Babette's Feast is a parable of grace, of course, and even the hardest heart might melt when all is said and done. More than just the story of one woman's love for people who have been ungrateful, it is really about what Martin Luther meant when he said that to be a Christian is to love God and "sin boldly."[1] The sect members are so trapped in the past that when freedom is offered to them—literally—on a plate, one of their number initially responds by saying, "I'm fearful of my joy." Their terror of the unknown and guilt for the past have left them doomed to only repeat words that have been dead for generations. Even the soldier is filled with regret; he abandoned a woman he loved to advance in the army, where he rose through the ranks and had an "honorable" career. But now, reminded of his former love, he asks, "Could many years of victory be seen as a defeat?" Babette introduces the one ingredient—sacrificial love—that helps them raise their sight line above themselves. In the near-hallucinogenic haze of the food and wine, they discover hidden depths of grace within themselves. And in the moonlight after the meal, they dance, rediscovering not only their wonder but their very humanity. And the reality of a relationship with Love breathes in them again.

Babette's Feast might cause you to reflect on your own need for a renewing desert experience or, conversely, the need to come out of the desert for a good feed. Bombarded by information, images, and noise that distort our sense of time and place, we may lose our sense of taste, and perhaps that's the same thing as losing our way. We look for certainties to hold amid the not knowing where to turn and seeing too many terrifying things on our phones and TVs. Wedded to religious or political ideologies that speak words (*grace* or *freedom*, for instance) without tasting them, never mind knowing how to live them, we can become convinced that our beliefs, our stories, are healing us because other people seem to feel the same way. The emperor's new clothes can be ideas too.

▲▼▲

I asked a radical clergyman once what he thought the solution was to the challenges of the northern Ireland of my youth, where legalistic stiffness has coexisted with mutual enmity and even violence, although grace has continually broken through. The clergyman said, "The solution is the hard gospel. The hard gospel is not that you don't say the F-word or that you don't sleep with your girlfriend before you're married. The hard gospel is that you love God and love your neighbor as yourself. End of story." I know that this may rankle some. But he's right. This is Babette's modus operandi too. Her gift to the dormant community is to awaken them to say, "Little children, love one another." That's the hard gospel, and whether or not we call it that, it may be all we need.

Babette's Feast is a film about priorities: about where you should put yourself, what you should do with your beliefs and with your life, and what you should do with it once you get there. There may be no more loving act than giving a glass of cold water to a thirsty stranger; and of course if the glass is full of amontillado bought with a lottery ticket you could have used to purchase a different way of life, all the more so. Having said that, Babette knows that the Parisian scene isn't all it's cracked up to be; she grants access to that truth for the poor folks she has come to live with and reminds the old soldier of what really mattered about his past—not fashionable piety but being seen by another and truly seeing them.

▲▼▲

You can experience an entire lifetime in a single day, eternity in a moment.

Such experiences can be crushing, later on, if we don't know how to integrate the peaks of life with the mundane, the spectacular with what Kathleen has called the quotidian mysteries. Many people seem to be lost in permanent grief for the story of a prior utopian state that was never meant to last. Many, too, don't know how to experience miracles when they are actually happening.

Babette is teaching the community, and perhaps also herself, that everyday life is truly magical. The shaking of hands, the stirring of soup, the expression of gratitude, the singing of a simple song, the sipping of a single small glass of red wine at the end of a sweaty kitchen shift—all these are as *good* as welcoming a stranger, falling in love, or winning the lottery.

Babette's vision of life makes me think of the astonishing mantra of awe-liberation-pleasure activist adrienne maree brown, for me an elaboration on "Love God and do what you want." I like to think it is also a sketch of what the islanders in *Babette's Feast* might do the morning after the feast: "Where we are born into privilege, we are charged with dismantling any myth of supremacy. Where we are born into struggle, we are charged with claiming our dignity, joy and liberation."[2] Privilege and struggle are inevitable ingredients of life. If we don't learn what to do with them, privilege will corrode us and struggle exhaust us. People like Babette are gifted at helping others discern how to serve from their gifts and ask for what they need. Sometimes people like Babette show this without words. Some spiritual wisdom figures know that they will always receive even in the act of self-giving love. Cultivating an inner Babette would mean sharing our portion of light to heal the people around us, but it wouldn't mean rejecting the healing they can offer us. At the end of *Babette's Feast*, we have reason to hope that

Babette has not only found a permanent place of shelter but has actually given the community a recipe for becoming one she not only needs but wants.

Kathleen

I have a somewhat different take than Gareth on the meaning of *Babette's Feast*. I believe it is a parable about what happens to people of faith—in any religion—when they become extremely isolated, both physically and spiritually, and are led by an individual whose rules and regulations become draconian over time. In this film, that person is a pastor serving a dwindling group of Pietistic Lutherans on the remote west coast of Denmark's Jutland peninsula. As his group aged, he selfishly prevented his two lovely daughters from marrying so that they could help him keep the congregation going. And, grateful for the many works of charity these women provided the townspeople before and after their father's death—feeding the poorest among them and giving them their hand-knit socks and caps—the congregation had accepted the pastor's cruel oppression of his daughters, as they accepted much that he had taught them.

Pietism, a movement within the Lutheran Church that emerged in the late seventeenth century, emphasized personal devotion and trying to live a good Christian life. Its hymns contained words such as those the Jutland people sing: "Only when we have achieved sinless perfection can we be happy." In its worst form pietism devolved into xenophobia, leading people to fear and reject the outside world and the people in it. That is what one might expect from this film's villagers when strangers appear. But it's not what we get.

Given the mutual distrust between Roman Catholics and Protestants in the nineteenth century, the capacity of these

Pietists to open their hearts and offer hospitality to two French Catholics—Achille, a well-known singer from the Paris Opera, and Babette, who will eventually be revealed as a renowned Parisian chef—is astonishing. It is as if, despite their world-renouncing theology, these folks have taken the deepest message of the Christian gospel to heart: to love God means to love one's neighbor as oneself. To my mind these people reveal themselves to be Christian humanists of the first order.

Professional singing was not a reputable career in the nineteenth century, and social norms dictated that women would not work outside the home. It is remarkable to see the town grocer and his wife renting a room in their home to the singer. And on the stormy night when Babette appears, struggling to walk upright in a fierce wind, the pastor's two daughters welcome this weary refugee who appears at their door. She speaks French, not their native tongue, and is so exhausted it seems that she can't take another step. The sisters offer her coffee, warm, dry clothing, and a place to stay. The film asks us if we would do the same.

I believe that the incredibly generous gesture Babette makes in preparing the villagers an extravagant meal with her unexpected lottery win is not, as some have interpreted it, a great cook offering repressed, abstemious fools a sumptuous meal. Babette's generosity is a response to the generous welcome she has received, not only from the two sisters but from all the villagers.

Having fled the bloodshed of the 1871 Paris Commune rebellion in which her husband and son had been killed, Babette has settled in a quiet place and come to herself again. She has not forgotten who she is and feels compelled to add fresh herbs to the awful-looking bread-and-ale soup the sisters prepare for elderly shut-ins. The recipients of the flavor-enhanced soup notice the difference and are not about to complain.

Gareth feels that the villagers have lost the meaning of the words of Scripture they recite, but their actions say otherwise. And I disagree with him about the sound of their singing. It is clear from their faces that singing with enthusiasm brings these people joy. They, along with their pastor, may have forgotten that St. Paul listed joy as one of the fruits of the Spirit. But as the music of their hymns inhabits their bodies, their faces cannot help revealing the pleasure it's giving them.

Any small religious community, especially one dominated by a single individual for a long time, faces a serious test when that person dies. Many communities don't survive. It is not surprising that after the death of their founder, the people in this little group begin quarreling. Grudges nursed for years surface and people feel free to berate each other. While the congregation admires the sisters, it doesn't give them the respect it gave their father. Distressed to hear harsh reprimands and old accusations being made around their table even when they try to lead the group in worship, the sisters become flustered. But Babette, who knows from bitter experience that hateful sentiments can lead to acts of violence, is having none of it. She expects better of these people and lets them know it. They listen and obey.

There is much delicious comedy in this film, none of it trivial. When Achille attends a Lutheran church service—surprising for a nineteenth-century Roman Catholic—he notices that one young woman has an exceptional voice and asks her father's permission to offer singing lessons. I expected that this man—the congregation's pastor—would refuse and was surprised when he did not. Singing was evidently important to him as a means of worshiping God. But when Achille and the girl rehearse the passionate seduction scene from *Don Giovanni*, it proves to be too much, not only for the father but for the naive young woman as well.

We laugh at the villagers' growing consternation over the exotic ingredients for Babette's feast as they are carried in a long procession from a small boat on the seashore to the sisters' kitchen. Seeing the bottles of wine and champagne, large quantities of eggs, small birds in a cage, and even a live turtle, they ask themselves if they are being tempted by the devil. They will not insult Babette or the sisters by refusing to attend the meal, but they resolve to make no comment on the food. This results in hilarity, as the one person who recognizes each gourmet dish, a worldly soldier who has brought his mother to the dinner, expecting drab fare, cannot help remarking on the excellent quality of the food and wine. The villagers respond with comments about the weather.

But as the evening progresses, once again, as with their energetic singing, it is the people's faces that give them away. Aglow with Babette's fine food and wine, they also glow with bonhomie and begin to openly express their affection for one another. Old lovers reunite; old wounds are healed. As they leave their quarreling in the past, I sense that we are being asked to look at ourselves to discern what it takes for us to abandon our own grudges and anger. Sharing a meal can help, but we need the spirit of hospitality, generosity, and self-sacrifice exemplified by Babette and the sisters.

Maybe it's because I have been a Benedictine oblate for many years, but *Babette's Feast* keeps returning me to the theme of hospitality. The Rule of St. Benedict asks monks to receive all guests as if they were Christ. In the film we see how hospitality breeds more hospitality until Wisdom herself sits with these folks as they share a feast, and the Holy Spirit breathes life into their weary souls.

The film exemplifies another core monastic value, one that predates the Benedictines. From its earliest days, 1,700 years ago in the deserts of the Middle East, monks have stood firm against the temptation to judge others. This can be a temptation for contemporary people watching *Babette's Feast*. But if we raise theological objections to the pietism of this small band of Christians and sneer at their attempts to repress their pleasure as they eat Babette's meal, we are missing the point of the film. And similarly, we are being self-indulgent if we apply today's standards to Babette's menu and condemn her killing of a turtle to make soup.

I hope that the film inspires us to see its characters as flawed human beings, much like ourselves. I'm interested that the words of Psalm 85, an apparent favorite of the pastor and recited by his congregation even after his death, surface several times in the film: "Mercy and faithfulness have met; justice and peace have embraced" (v. 11).[3]

These words represent a vision of a future that only love and hospitality can bring about. But in the psalm, they come after a bitter lament, the people suffering from such trauma that they ask God, "Will you be angry with us forever, will your anger never cease?" (v. 6). The psalm continues with a prayer to be restored, and suddenly a voice of hope emerges, asserting that God speaks of peace and insisting that "his help is near to those who fear him" (v. 10).[4] This is fear in the sense of holy awe rather than dread. It is the awe that overcomes the much-decorated soldier who in his youth had been vain, ambitious, and self-serving. Now he ponders the lack of love in his life and asks, "Could many years of victory be seen as a defeat?" It is the awe we all experience as we take stock of the choices we've made in our lives and where they have led us. We may harbor regrets over what might have been, but if we've ever witnessed a coming together of kindness and justice, or have found a simple joy in doing what is right, we might join Babette in raising a glass of Veuve Clicquot and making a toast to all the treasures life has offered us, often despite ourselves.

Questions and Conversations

1. Does anyone in your life remind you of Babette?
2. Have you, like the island community, experienced religion without spirit?
3. Have you had an experience of dead or dormant religion or beliefs being transformed into something life-giving?
4. Where do you need someone like Babette to help heal you, as an individual and in community?
5. Inspired by Babette, what is an extravagant gift you could share with others?
6. Have you ever received hospitality in the form of an unexpected grace that changed your life?
7. Are there treasures that have come to you despite yourself?
8. Looking at the quote from Psalm 85:11, would you say that mercy and truth come together for the villagers and Babette?
9. Do "what if" questions trouble you? Do you wonder about what your life would be if you had made different choices? If so, how do you answer those questions and live with them?

10

TRANSFORMING CONFLICT

> **Wonder Woman 1984 (USA, 2020)**
>
> Directed by Patty Jenkins, written by Patty Jenkins, Geoff Johns, and Dave Callaham
>
> An ancient Amazonian princess and a Reagan-era entrepreneur in early midlife struggle with the tension between getting what each wants for themself and what the world most needs.

Gareth

Wonder Woman 1984 (WW84) may be the most spiritually sophisticated of the superhero movies, a beautiful genre hybrid about second chances. Director Patty Jenkins and her fantastic star, Gal Gadot, take the role as seriously as if she were playing Gandhi, and they made a film full of fun and excitement that says something I've wanted to hear a movie say almost since I started watching them. It's an often hilarious satire of 1980s action movies, sexism, and individualism; a tremendously entertaining action movie in itself; a story for everyone that centers a woman; and, most of all, a movie that's honest about love, ambition, regret, grief, and responding to conflict without making it worse.

To anyone who might think it's asking too much of a comic book blockbuster to speak to the needs of our real lives, I'd offer two things. The first is from Lex Luthor in the first *Superman* (a reference for *WW84*). From his elegant lair beneath Grand Central Station, Luthor says something almost biblical in its philosophical depth: "Some people can read *War and Peace* and come away thinking it's just a simple adventure story. Other people can read the back of a chewing gum wrapper and unlock the secrets of the universe." A movie's genre should not determine whether it can speak to our lives. Rather than dismissing a movie as having little to say because it has lots of special effects or moves quickly, we should ask whether it is made with a humane consciousness. *WW84* is certainly that.

The second thing is that growing up I was immersed in a story of violent conflict and a story of making peace. What I came to believe is that the story we tell—and the way we tell it—will shape what we believe to be possible in the world and the role we can play in it. Sometimes what we need is a consciously serious engagement with the most challenging or even horrific circumstances, such as *Schindler's List*, *12 Years a Slave*, *Raging Bull*, or *Nomadland*. Sometimes we need nonnarrative art to speak more ineffably, to help us feel, or to meet us in feelings that are overwhelming or numbing. (I think of *Hiroshima Mon Amour*, *Koyaanisqatsi*, and *Baraka*.) And sometimes we need to step into the mythical to discover more of who we really are.

Now, I can't fly, and I don't wear a red cape, but I do sometimes feel a bit alien to the world, and it seems to me that part of the spiritual path is to discover your own kryptonite (or besetting vulnerabilities) and learn what to do with it. I don't dress up like a bat or have an armored car, but I do want to care for the city in which I live, to serve its needs from the abundance of gifts and privileges that I did not earn, and when my truest self is awake I recognize that sometimes service may result in being scapegoated and that it's good to learn not to seek credit. I don't have a Lasso of Truth, nor can I spin very fast, but I do experience empathy for the needs of those around me and a growing sense that if the power to tell a story can shape our lives, then storytellers have an essential responsibility to discern the truest and most helpful version of the stories we're telling. And being forged in an experience of witnessing conflict and suffering, I find it both necessary and sometimes even easy to delight in good things in a way that some people might call naive. Today has enough pain and struggle to concern us; we don't need to add to it by denying that the world is also beautiful.

What's most thrilling to me about *Wonder Woman 1984*, and the primary reason it's in this book, is that both what the heroine does to save the world and why the villain creates the need to save it are presented as being entirely understandable, entirely imitable, and entirely human.

That's what I yearn for in stories that claim to have something to teach. For a human to relate to a superhero, the superhero must have qualities that parallel our own capacities. The same goes for depictions of historical figures. Stories about heroes—whether from outer space or across the street—that present them as having magical powers or merely being in the right place at the right time, with the right attitude, aren't of much use to me. I live in a body and a world that (mostly) doesn't need magical powers anyway—while a selfless person stepping in front of a train to rescue an endangered child is an actual thing that sometimes happens in the world, such occasions are extremely rare. What's more often needed, and readily available, is the ability to tell a story that invites people to look up from their lives and take a step toward being enlarged by love. There may be nothing more powerful than a story, and *Wonder Woman 1984* knows this.

Its own storytelling is marvelous, rooted in Diana's inner monologue, remembering her childhood as something that "feels so very far away, and other [times] I can almost see it." It begins with an invocation of how our childhood dreams felt like promises, then immediately presents an example of how there are no shortcuts to authentic growth. Cheating won't get us what we want. Indeed, what we think we want may not be what we need or even what we want after all. The point of *WW84* is outlined in that first sequence as a mother figure tells Diana, "Greatness is not what you think."

It's a magnificent spectacle that inspires awe—a horse jumping over a chasm, Diana's first time in an airplane, the open road chase, and Diana later flying under her own skill. But most of all there is Diana's realization that her physical prowess is not enough to defeat the evil expanding exponentially in the person of Max Lord (a fantastic name for a bad guy, fabulously played by Pedro Pascal). Most action movies have the hero simply kill the villain, often with an extra magic weapon appearing out of nowhere at the last minute. There's rarely any acknowledgment of the aftermath of killing—both for the victim and for the person responsible. A few movie heroes, to be sure, take steps to minimize casualties, but Wonder Woman goes as far as ensuring that the brakes still work on a henchman's truck. The evolution of the principles of self-defense and just war theory embodied in the most effective conflict transformation practices advocate more than merely not killing each other; we must do unto others as we would have them do unto us. Wonder Woman is trying very hard to do that. She is not weak, but brave.

A musician was once asked why he was playing his cello on the streets of Sarajevo as bombs dropped. His response is another way of reminding us that, as Richard Rohr says, "the best criticism of the bad is the practice of the better."[1] The story is told different ways, but the one I've heard has the cellist saying something like, *The question should not be why am I playing my cello as bombs drop, but why are they dropping bombs while I play my cello?*

We can choose to do the creative thing, the community thing, the life-giving thing, and the impossible thing, even when the option of doing the scapegoating thing, the selfish thing, the separating and death-dealing thing, the same as usual thing is right before us. It's not that the life-giving thing has been attempted and failed but rather that we are programmed to let other people decide for us, and our culture is dominated by oppositional stories as if they were the way things must always be.

Our very vision of life is a story that can kill us or enlarge us—not in opposition to or competition with others but as part of the light that can heal them too. WW84 heals by telling the truth that if our deepest wishes are obstacles to the holy dreams of others, then renouncing those wishes would be a heroic act. To forgo selfishness and individualism in favor of acting for a world in which everyone has what they need is not a tragedy and perhaps not even a sacrifice. Of course sometimes giving up a wish is desperately painful—and the scene where Diana and her boyfriend, Steve Trevor, part takes such pain seriously. It happens quickly—from the realization that Diana and Steve's fantasy of withdrawing from the world has become part of the problem, to one of the most moving farewell kisses in cinema history, to Diana learning how to fly. The visual fluidity of that sequence is astonishing. But it's the portrayal of the stages of grief that strikes me the most. With tears, Diana remembers Steve's words about how to join with the air, and she lets his presence guide her. This is what healing grief looks like—when the gift of the person who has gone is now somehow a part of us. When we more fully embody the gifts that were awakened by a loved one who has now died, somehow the person lives again.

It's at this point, when Diana has stepped out of an unhealthy fantasy and into her truer self, when she has integrated a painful memory with its gift, that she can finally save the world. And it's here where *WW84* has something profound to say about dealing with conflict. Exhausted in the corner after discovering that she cannot overpower the villain physically (because oppositional energy always recreates itself), Wonder Woman leads from Diana's heart. No fireworks, just the authority of words that tell a truth big enough to include everyone.

It's a brief speech that could be or *should* be given on the floor of Congress, or at least every church, synagogue, mosque, or temple, or when appearing on a talk show or at a grocery store checkout, buying a bus ticket, interviewing for a job, or sitting down for dinner with family. The culminating words in *WW84* could have been written by the peace workers in the place where I'm from, or anywhere that people have needed to move beyond stories of separation, selfishness, and scapegoating.

This world was a beautiful place just as it was, but you cannot have it all. You can only have the truth, and the truth is enough. The truth is beautiful. Look at this world and look at what your wish is costing it. You must be the hero. Only you can save the day. Renounce your wish if you want to save this world.

Because you're not the only one who has suffered, who wants more, who wants them back, who doesn't want to be afraid anymore. Or alone. Or frightened. Or powerless.

Because you're not the only one who imagined a world where everything was different, better, finally. A world where they were loved, and seen, and appreciated, finally.

But what is it costing you? Do you see the truth?

Effective conflict transformation doesn't deny the need for belonging and safety. The problem arises when my way of claiming belonging and safety diminishes the legitimate belonging and safety of others. Dealing with conflict doesn't deny the legitimate needs of the people involved. It just helps us all find ways to meet those needs without harming each other.

It may take a long time to learn the difference between needs and wants, never mind to develop a sense of self that connects me to every human and the rest of the ecosystem too. Apparently Wonder Woman is about five thousand years old, and even she hasn't been perfected yet. But she understands something we need to learn. That something is the grace that comes when you renounce your selfish desires in favor of wanting the most good for everyone and everything. It is the only answer to the stories that keep us separate and conceive of the world as a battle between two kinds of people, one of whom must be disempowered, defeated, or even eradicated. Those stories threaten to destroy us all.

But if we listen to the wisdom in this movie, the possibility of the world our most whole selves dream of becomes clear and magnetic. A world in which we would just love each other, and no one would have to make a wish for that. A world in which no one would be humiliated or have to beg for the scraps of dignity, in which offering mercy would be seen as a sign of strength. A world in which every conversation could be an opportunity to call forth the best in each other. Where everyone would live, to paraphrase one sacred text, beneath their vine and fig tree, in peace and unafraid (Mic. 4:4).

But as the Talmud has it, whoever saves one life saves the world entire. So you don't have to be a superhero to save the world (nor do you need to save the world to be a superhero). Loving one person well may be the most you can do. The trick may be to recognize that each person you meet is also a facet of the person you already care about the most. And to love strangers is also to love your most cherished friend. Even better, to love strangers is another way of loving ourselves. (For what it's worth, that doesn't mean we have to get rid of boundaries—even Wonder Woman has to show Barbara/Cheetah some tough love, but only after she's tried everything else, and she apologizes for the pain it's going to cause.)

Wonder Woman is my favorite comic book hero, at least in this iteration, because she's *relatable* and actually offers something we can emulate. She is color and joy, courage and vulnerability, and it is her most human qualities that make the most difference.

It's difficult to make a movie that tells the truth without seeming didactic—to achieve a tone that moves from light to dark and back again, that presents deep ideas on an entertaining ride, that has the main character and the villain both grow. What's most amazing about *WW84* is that if we pay attention to what it's really saying, we will grow too. Just thinking about it makes me want to love more.

Kathleen

Watching *Wonder Woman 1984*, I think of those among our readers who are over sixty years of age and rarely watch movies. Their only exposure to a superhero film is likely to come when they are accompanying their grandchildren, and they may find it odd to find Gareth taking a Wonder Woman film so seriously. But I would encourage them to engage with his insight into the film's treatment of the subjects of self-sacrificial love and using one's gifts unselfishly for the benefit of others. He's right to ask us to consider the wisdom of this movie and its vision of "a world in which no one would be humiliated or have to beg for the scraps of dignity, in which offering mercy would be seen as a sign of strength."

But people who were not raised on the superhero movies of the DC or Marvel universe may feel that these messages are better conveyed in films with fewer CGI stunts. Some movies reach easily across generational boundaries to delight people old and young. I had always considered *The Wizard of Oz* to be such a film, and I believe that it is. But I recently ran across a comment by the filmmaker John Waters, who was astonished to hear a young person dismiss it as a ho-hum movie that was mostly about people walking. And walking.

This tells me that it is wise to always keep in mind that enjoying any film is a matter of personal taste and that one's age can weigh significantly in the matter. I hope Gareth's fine essay about the themes of *Wonder Woman 1984* will convince all our readers that the film is worth their time and attention.

I agree with many of the critics who found that, as often happens in film franchises, much of the charm of the 2017 *Wonder Woman* was lost in the second movie, which feels overstuffed. Gal Gadot as Diana still brings considerable wit and humor to her role, letting us know with a wink that she doesn't take herself or her superpowers too seriously. She's aided by Kristen Wiig and Pablo Pascal, who provide a good dose of both pathos and comedy, chewing up the scenery in their roles as a resentful frenemy and an ambitious man whose desire to rule the world is fueled by his fear of being labeled a loser. Max Lord is the perfect name for a man weakened by self-doubt who becomes a megalomaniac, and Barbara Minerva, as a gemologist at the Smithsonian, comes to represent the dual aspects of the Roman goddess of both wisdom and war. We can see ourselves in their faults, their motives, and their steep learning curve as they are called to recognize what truly matters in this world. Ironically, it's the otherworldly Wonder Woman who provides them with the necessary reality check.

For people who might not catch all this film's references to 1980s superhero movies, such as the *Superman* film Gareth cites, his valuable insight into the "humane consciousness" of this film can steer us to a better understanding of what makes *Wonder Woman 1984* so different from the many films in which the good folks "win" by obliterating the bad ones. The nonstop kindness Wonder Woman offers to both innocent children and enemies who are trying to kill her is remarkable. Her refusal to destroy Max Lord, but instead to implore him to rediscover his humanity, is the true wonder of the film. As Max finally accepts the unconditional love of his young son, the movie insists (if a bit too loudly and with one too many explosions) that only love can transform us and break through our fever dreams of gaining power over others in our desire to always have "more." I was less satisfied by where we find Barbara Minerva as the movie ends. As she morphed into Cheetah, Wonder Woman's archenemy in the

DC world, I felt that it was the franchise that was winning the battle.

Wonder Woman, by far the most popular female comic book character ever made, first appeared in a 1942 comic book in which a journalist describes her as "psychological propaganda for the new type of woman who, I believe, should rule the world." Her inventor, William Moulton Marston, was a psychologist who felt that during World War II, he needed to create a character bent on reconciling people. And I can attest that despite early criticism by the National Organization for Decent Literature that Wonder Woman "is not sufficiently dressed," young girls today are inspired by her scanty costume. When my grand-nieces dress as Wonder Woman for Halloween, they stand a little taller and are perhaps wishing that the golden lasso that can rope others into telling the truth is for real.

Even though this film is set in the 1980s, it has great relevance for us. In its thrilling opening sequence of a competition between women in Diana's native culture, we hear a mother figure warn the young Diana, who has tried to win by cheating, that "no true hero is born of lies" and that "greatness is not what you think." Her admonition and subsequent developments, especially Max Lord's attempts to become the most powerful man in the world, remind us that we have grown far too accustomed to lying and cheating as a way of life, especially in the realms of politics and business. Wonder Woman allows us to imagine a world in which winning does not mean puffing up one's ego by insulting others or gaslighting the public with "alternative facts."

Wonder Woman 1984 offers valuable insight into what constitutes greatness, especially when we are threatened by conflict and danger. Listen to Gareth here: "The evolution of the principles of self-defense and just war theory embodied in the most effective conflict transformation practices advocate more than merely not killing each other; we must do unto others as we would have them do unto us. Wonder Woman is trying very hard to do that. She is not weak, but brave."

The film is unusual in that it gives us a superhero whose impressive powers are failing her. Diana's love for her long-lost pilot, Steve, has distracted her, and only when she renounces what she wants most in the world, that they might be reunited forever, does she regain the strength to save the world by helping others transform themselves. In her final encounter with Max, she can't lasso him into the truth but must plead with him, relying on the power of words alone. It is a remarkable speech, one that Gareth rightly insists should be repeated everywhere and often. I'm glad he quotes it in its entirety and am grateful that such a message is offered in a blockbuster so that millions can hear it. The questions Wonder Woman raises are questions we need to ask ourselves, everywhere and often, as we pursue what we want at the expense of other people and the planet itself: *But what is it costing you? Do you see the truth?*

While Gareth rightly appreciates *Wonder Woman 1984*'s honesty "about love, ambition, regret, grief, and responding to conflict without making it worse," I much prefer movies about conflict and reconciliation that feature human beings and not fictional superheroes. Two that come to mind are *The Best of Enemies* and *Of Gods and Men*. The first, starring Sam Rockwell and Taraji P. Henson, tells the true story of C. P. Ellis, a man who renounced his role as a leader in the Ku Klux Klan. As he developed a friendship with an African American activist named Ann Atwater, the two of them worked to desegregate public schools in their native Durham, North Carolina.

The second is a French film, *Of Gods and Men*. It's another true story and concerns a small community of Cistercian monks in rural Algeria during a time of civil unrest. We witness the deep friendships that the monks had developed with their neighbors in an impoverished Muslim village, trying as best they can to provide them with medical care and necessities like shoes. Several monks, including the abbot, speak Arabic, have studied the Koran, and enjoy visiting with the local imam.

The townspeople warn the monks of increased violence by armed rebels who seek to establish an Islamic state, and after Serbian road construction workers the monks had befriended are suddenly attacked and murdered, it becomes clear that the monks are also at risk. Government officials offering military protection are refused, the abbot stating, "That is not an option."

The monks deal courageously with armed guerrillas who appear at their gate, the abbot calmly but firmly insisting that they leave their weapons outside. Not long after a rebel leader who had come to respect the monks is killed by the Algerian army, another group attacks the monastery and kidnaps the men. In the closing credits we learn that the monks' bodies were discovered on May 21, 1996. We also learn that two monks who had managed to hide during the kidnapping survived to tell the story depicted in the film.

In one of the community's conversations about whether the men should remain with the townspeople or depart, one observes that in becoming monks they had already given up their lives in the service of others. The men agree that staying in place makes sense, even at the cost of their lives.

It was later learned that the abbot, Christian de Chergé, had sent a letter forgiving his future assassins to his mother in France. Opened after his murder, it read in part, "I would like, when the time comes, to have a space of clearness that would allow me to beg forgiveness of God and of my fellow human beings, and at the same time to forgive with all my heart the one who will strike me down. . . . My death . . . will appear to confirm those who hastily judged me naive or idealistic . . . but they should know that for this life lost, I give thanks to God. In this 'thank you' . . . I certainly include you, my last-minute friend who will not have known what you are doing. . . . I commend you to the God in whose face I see yours. And may we find each other, happy 'good thieves' in Paradise, if it please God, the Father of us both."

An ordinary man, called to live in an extraordinary way, rendering an indelible witness to the power of love to conquer hatred and death. That is a superhero in my book.

Questions and Conversations

1. What wishes have you been told to believe are legitimate?
2. How might your wishes be obstacles to the dreams of others?
3. How might the wishes of others be obstacles to your dreams?
4. When have you taken shortcuts in life that turned out not to work?
5. How could you enlarge your sense of self to include others?
6. What is one thing you would do to renounce selfish wishes in favor of a world in which everyone's legitimate needs are met?

7. Have you experienced grief integrating with a memory of a loved one becoming part of who you are today?

8. How can your dreams for yourself bring about a world in which everyone would live in peace and unafraid?

11

DEATH AND BEYOND

After Life (Japan, 1998)

Directed and written by Hirokazu Kore-eda

People from all walks of life make their eternity from the memory of the most loving moment they can recall. They allow the knowledge of their death to bring them life, showing the power of cinema to stir us to the same.

Kathleen

I envy anyone watching this movie for the first time. It's a quiet film, but it is best for the viewer to remain alert and not be lulled by the film's gentle pace or intriguing characters into thinking that you fully understand what's going on. We see people arriving, one by one, at a decrepit schoolhouse, and as a bell rings in the fog we wonder, who are these people, and what has brought them together? They are elderly and young and in between, and would seem to have little in common, yet they converse enthusiastically until a woman with a clipboard enters the room and apologizes for keeping them waiting. Then, as she calls each person by name, she explains that she is assigning them a room and a counselor.

We then see a young man sitting at a desk greet an elderly woman as she enters a classroom. Smiling, she sits in a chair opposite him, and he tells her that he must follow protocol and make sure she understands why she is there. "You died yesterday," he says, adding, "I'm sorry for your loss." The woman nods, still smiling, and says calmly, "I'm so sorry." We sense that wherever she finds herself, her instinct is to establish good relationships, to cooperate and not cause difficulty for others.

And with that, we are off and running into the afterlife. This woman's pleasant demeanor is one key to appreciating the film. It is not about death or even an imagined afterlife so much as it is about the lives we have lived and how we might come to view them after they have ended. In an interview, director Hirokazu Kore-eda explains that in Japanese, the title of the film means "wonderful life." He is no doubt aware of the 1946 American classic, *It's a Wonderful Life*, in which Jimmy Stewart plays a despairing man who is allowed to see what his family and town would have been like had he never lived. In an odd way, both films look more into the future than the past. But *After Life* is not in any sense a remake of the older movie. We see no flashbacks; instead, we hear people tell stories about the lives they have lived.

The counselors explain to the newcomers that their job is to help them choose the one memory they will take with them into eternity. They have three days for this task. The counselors will act as guides, and once the newcomers have made their choice the staff will attempt to create the memory on film. Immediately after they have viewed it, they will enter the afterlife. The counselors' conversations with the people as they choose a memory offer the film's most delightful moments.

This film has enchanted me ever since I first saw it, not only because this assignment caused me to reflect on what memory I would select but also because of the great privilege offered these recently deceased people. Wouldn't any of us, in this life or the next, welcome being encouraged by sympathetic people to talk about our lives in a way that helps us put them into perspective?

We begin to recognize ourselves in some of these people and feel sorry for those who claim that they have nothing worth remembering. But other memories are inspiring. A veteran of World War II talks of being surrounded by American troops when he and his fellow soldiers were starving and suffering terribly from a lack of salt. He figured he was going to be shot anyway, so he asked for a cigarette and was surprised when a GI gave him one. He doesn't want to ever forget the kindness of the American soldiers who fed their prisoners rice laced with life-giving salt.

One of my favorite people in the film is a sweet-faced elderly woman who does not answer her counselor's questions. She may have dementia, but her wise expression and self-contained demeanor suggest otherwise. She simply chooses not to talk, except when she goes to the window and asks if the cherry trees outside will ever blossom. That question gives us a key to her personality and the memory she will eventually choose.

The counselors may joke about a client who speaks incessantly about all the sex he had in his life—and he provides the most preposterous memories in the film—but when a person is sitting in front of them, the counselors do not judge. They listen. One man talks about a suicide attempt he almost made when he was in his twenties, then describes

the ordinary but beautiful thing that stopped him. A flirta-
tious middle-aged woman, the veteran of many affairs, says
that she was a romantic at heart, but true love eluded her.
The memory she selects is one of the most poignant in the
film, but I missed its significance the first time I saw *After
Life*. I wondered why anyone would choose the memory of
simply waiting in a hotel room for a lover to arrive. While
this woman sometimes lies, if you have been listening to her
carefully, her choice is unutterably sad, but it makes sense.

It's easy to get lost in these characters and their stories,
but as the film reveals itself slowly, it is important to keep
asking questions. Who are the counselors, and why are they
working here? This becomes significant as the staff, rather
than those they serve, become the movie's focus. One scene
in particular merits close attention. A young counselor, Mochizuki, has been struggling to help a man who died in his
seventies select a memory. In their discussion of Japanese
social attitudes toward marriage, Mochizuki refers to "our
generation." That "our" is essential in understanding the
rest of the film.

After Life rewards repeated viewings. Much of its deceptive simplicity comes from its matter-of-fact narrative style.
Kore-eda chose as his cinematographer Yutaka Yamazaki, an
experienced documentarian who insisted on using a handheld camera, which makes us feel that we're not watching
fiction but real life. It also frees Kore-eda from the cliched
clouds, dreamy soft-focus, and mawkish, sentimental over-
kill that we find in many films about life after death, such
as *Ghost* or *What Dreams Will Come*. No glitz or glamour
here: the waystation on the road to eternity in *After Life* is
a dingy schoolhouse with peeling paint.

There is another reason for the film's realistic tone. Kore-
eda has said that he was inspired to make it after he and

his assistants had conducted interviews with more than five hundred elderly people about their views of death and the afterlife. He found their stories so moving that he asked a number of those interviewed if they'd be willing to be in his film. *After Life* has excellent professional actors in its cast, but there are also eleven ordinary people who said yes to Kore-eda's invitation.

The elements of Japanese culture that appear in the film are mostly self-explanatory, and we can determine from the context what they mean. When a woman offers a childhood memory of the Great Kanto earthquake of 1923, she had been too young to be aware of the terrible devastation it caused. (The quake and subsequent fires killed 140,000 people.) Her memory is a happy one of playing with other children in the bamboo forest where her family had fled and of her mother making rice balls over a fire.

One woman speaks of praying before the shrine of her deceased brother, a common practice in the Shinto faith. Several characters mention having celebrated their "Adult Day" when they reached the age of eighteen. One of the counselors, Satoru, feels that he's doing his duty as a father by working at the waystation until his daughter, who was just three when he died, can celebrate her coming of age. Until then he is content to visit her on what he calls the Day of the Dead, or the Japanese Obon festival. It takes place every summer, when people welcome the spirits of their beloved deceased, honoring them with songs and dances. The one truly nasty remark in the film comes from a trainee counselor, Shiori, a wary and cynical teenager who does not seem to mind having died young as much as having had a difficult life with no father. When Satoru becomes exasperated with her, she warns him that she is what you get when a girl grows up without a father.

As the counselors and a crew (who were the actual crew of *After Life*) prepare to film the memories that the people have chosen, the movie's charm intensifies. The crew cuts cherry blossoms out of paper and, standing on ladders, shakes them out of baskets. They gently and rhythmically push against the side of an old bus for a man whose best memory is of riding a trolley as a young student. They make clouds out of cotton for a man who savors his memory of soloing in a Cessna. It is all delightfully homespun, a feeling that is reinforced as we hear the out-of-tune amateur band playing a march as they lead the group to the auditorium where they will watch the reenactments.

But through it all, a new and significant story is emerging. Shiori questions her colleagues, "What's the point of all our work?" She has grown more anxious as she's grown closer to Mochizuki and now senses that he will soon be leaving for the afterlife. During this week, one of the recently deceased has revealed something critically important to Mochizuki about his own life and a woman he had once loved. Kore-eda has said that he identifies with this character, who had felt that his memories were locked inside himself but has now learned that other people's memories are also a part of him. Mochizuki had long felt aimless and lost but can now say, "I was part of someone else's happiness; what a wonderful discovery." When Shiori responds by saying, "I can't bear to be forgotten by anyone else," Mochizuki offers her a convincing reassurance. At last, he is ready to have his memory filmed, a scene that as often as I see this film will always make me weep.

In interviews Kore-eda has said that he feels that sensing the presence of the dead is necessary for us to understand our life, and he often thinks about the way that pieces of our lives are held in the memories of others. In his love of ordinary people and of life itself he reminds me of Agnès Varda, another humanist whose work encourages us to reflect on who we are and what we need to make us happy and fulfilled. This beautiful film is not so much about death as time and human memory. It affirms that our lives, while fragile and transient, are a treasure so great that we are to take good care with ourselves and with everyone we meet.

After Life offers us an irresistible invitation to consider the one memory we would like to live with forever. I would want to be with my family, sitting at a table in our big house in Honolulu, where three generations of the clan lived for many years. My parents, who brought me into this world, would be there, along with my two sisters, my brother, and their spouses, and my three nieces and a nephew. We would all be enjoying each other's company and complimenting my husband on the magnificent Christmas dinner he had prepared. I could live forever on our conversation and our laughter.

Gareth

A retired archbishop once told me that if he had to do it all over again he would invite his clergy "to get out of their pulpits" and live "among the people." He was speaking of a place in which clericalism and patriarchy were taking a long time to loosen their grip. I think he overstated his earlier failures, but I knew why he felt able to say these things at that stage of his life. Variations on the theme often come from anyone nearing the end: people regret not living more freely, not speaking from the heart, not saying "I love you" more often, not figuring out what they really want and learning how to ask for it, not treasuring the little things, not caring for others, not slowing down, not doing what they know is right more than what is expedient or self-serving. Of course, sometimes people also rage against the dying of the light, wanting to hold on to what they cannot keep or to achieve something they cannot control; but regret for the past or denial about the future is a waste of spirit. *After Life*, a movie about death that loves life, shows the way beyond both.

Hirokazu Kore-eda was in his midthirties when he made *After Life*, and I was in my early twenties when I first saw it. I had recently had a confrontation with death, curled up on the floor of a concert hall in Australia, while punk violin played and I flash-forwarded to the future loss of my parents. The screeching strings seemed to tear open a curtain that had provided some protection, but now I was overcome with feeling alone and with dread that the people who had brought me into being would someday not be there. I think my psyche interpreted it as a signal that I would also not be "there." It was terrifying and lasted for months. But it eventually integrated itself, or at least settled enough to feel like detachment, not collapse. I needed a tender guide like Kore-eda to help me discern the difference between taking death seriously and taking myself too seriously. *After Life* helped me begin to embrace the life-giving properties of death awareness.

One of those properties is that if we accept that nothing lasts forever (at least in its current form), then the universal spiritual teaching to not worry about tomorrow is more easily practiced. If one of my tomorrows will inevitably be the last tomorrow, then what I concern myself with today may look very different.

After Life is about the newly deceased choosing a memory to live in for eternity, but it's equally about the ongoing journeys of the bureaucrats who serve them. They get to do for a living what Marina Abramović did in her performance piece titled *The Artist Is Present*: they sit in front of strangers, looking and listening deeply—perhaps the first time those strangers have felt heard and seen. The revelation that these officials are themselves in a waiting room, having not yet claimed a memory, is both moving and hopeful. Just as it may never be too early to start thinking meaningfully about death, our mentor Kore-eda, clearly an old and new soul at once, shows us the other side. It's never too late *to find a path to more life*, even if you think you're already dead.

I don't want to diminish the pain that many of us have witnessed or experienced in the deaths of people we love, especially not the suffering that often accompanies a long journey of profound illness. But I have also experienced how catastrophe calls forth love, how people run into burning buildings to protect the vulnerable, how some of us with little have shared it with others rather than hoarding it and have discovered in that sharing that the little we had somehow multiplies, how weeping in someone's arms provides a comfort that a happy hug never can.

And there are stories of people whose own deaths have helped them become the person they always wanted to be— or that their loved ones hoped they would be. "Let's not panic"—the last words spoken by a friend who had just encouraged his spouse to pursue a path of liberation and love after his death—"because you have your journey, and I have mine." *After Life* asks us not to panic. It knows of wars and rumors of war, of broken relationships and of letters sent but not received. It knows that sometimes it can take decades to learn to look up from our lives and consider the light—and the needs—in the face of another.

It knows most of all that there are essential moments— literally moments in which the *essence* of life is revealed: a quiet hour on a park bench with a heart about to burst, a hand held by a person who helped us feel safe, the way the first time in an airplane might feel like being united with spirit. Of course I have pondered what memory I might take into the afterlife, every time I've watched the movie, for over half my life now.

▲▼▲

My maternal grandparents died on the same day, an hour apart. My paternal grandmother passed when my dad was two, my paternal grandfather when I was thirteen. I'm alive partly because my Jewish great-grandmother escaped pogroms in Eastern Europe more than eighty years or so before I was born. I grew up in a society where people were killing each other, fueled by political prejudice and aspirations. The story of death was part of the backdrop of my life.

Your story may be more or less dramatic. But we all came through a lot to get here, and a day will come when no one remembers us.

We spend so much time trying to fend off death, but if fears overcome our capacity to experience our souls, we risk never living at all. The best antidote is gratitude—not a feeling but a principle you claim—for the things for which you can authentically be thankful.

Living too close to an unhealthy story of death traumatizes some of us to the point of constant low-level fear. Many don't find the nurture they need or know how to ask for it. Some respond with misguided and destructive attempts to overcome death through asserting rage and dominance over others. But the path of creative acceptance and life-giving attention to the things that matter most is available to anyone who asks. We spend so much of our lives trying to avoid death when embracing it would be better. That is what will expand your horizons, not close them off.

I understand why Kathleen says *After Life* is not really a film about death, though I see it differently. For me it's about life lived in the light of a more whole appreciation of death, so perhaps it's best to say that it's about life and death together. As our perception of death is one of the most important influences on our perception of life, there's a way in which thinking about death can be the most life-giving thing. *After Life* is a movie about transforming disappointment with events by making an appointment *with* life. If we don't wake ourselves up from the nightmare imposed by unnecessary busyness, ego, careerism, the myth of redemptive violence, and zero-sum competition with our neighbors and enemies alike, our lives will be, at best, dominated by trivia (the enemy of experience) or, at worst, we'll get all the things we think we want but discover in the end we have nothing that matters.

The challenge, and the invitation, is to take steps to move past the sense of time slipping away, to *be in the moment you're in*—then, even a day of terrible weather can be a glorious one.

It seems so clear to me. The essence of life is love, and the way to experience this essence is to—simply and impossibly—do everything I can to notice and claim and fall into love. That means things that enable me to breathe more slowly and move toward union with self, others, and the beauty of the ecosystem. Maybe that sounds pretentious, so I'll put it another way: the way to truly experience love is to slow down, be with others, and look up from your life toward anything that brings light.

Reflecting on the welcoming light in *After Life*, the experience of watching and being healed by movies and by the conversation I have with them and others makes my path clear. Perhaps the memory I'd want to take into eternity, and inhabit forever, is of being in a cinema with spacious seating and—more importantly—gracious friends, watching this movie.

Questions and Conversations

1. Have you ever discovered that you meant more to another person than you ever could have guessed? What effect did that discovery have on you?

2. Is having a legacy or "evidence of your life" important to you?

3. Japanese culture considers our dead loved ones as presences that can be helpful and deserve our respect. Do you have this kind of relationship with deceased friends or family members?

4. Do you have memories that hold you back? Or memories that have freed you to move on with your life?

5. Kore-eda has stated that memory is "not a fossil, but ever-changing." Have you found that this is true for you?

6. What appeals to you about the idea of death being a kind of birth?

7. What memory might you take with you if you could live in this movie?

8. What would be different for you today if you lived into the experience you would like to take with you into eternity?

9. If you knew you had six months to live, what would you do differently? What's one step you could take, in the next week, to experience more of the life-giving properties of death awareness?

10. What is keeping you from finding the memory you most want to take with you?

11. If the path to maturity necessarily runs through the valley of immaturity, where can you show grace to yourself for your past mistakes?

12. What would it be like to experiment with saying "Good morning!" as if you really meant it?

13. If trivia is the enemy of experience, what's one thing you could do in the next day to exchange one for the other?

14. What matters most to you?

15. Can you imagine allowing yourself to be truly loved?

12

WAITING IN SILENCE

Into Great Silence (France/Switzerland/Germany, 2005)

Directed and written by Philip Gröning

A landmark documentary almost two decades in the making, exploring life in the cloistered Grand Chartreuse monastery of the Carthusian Order in France.

Kathleen

Perhaps only monks have the stamina and courage to wait in silence for what comes after death. But you don't need to be cloistered to appreciate that silence can be a marvelous gift to us. Movies are best appreciated in silence, but I have empirical evidence, dating from when I was a teenager, that if people are determined to talk during a film, they will sit near me.

I marvel at the extent to which people will go to avoid being silent when they're watching a movie they've paid good money to see. I once observed a young woman turn her back

143

to the screen so she could carry on an intense conversation with the man who was evidently her boyfriend. Many people feel compelled to offer inane comments on what they've just seen: "She walked into the room" or "That big man shot the smaller one." If their behavior annoys me enough, I will say, in a polite tone of voice, "Could you please stop talking? It's distracting." People usually seem so stunned by my request that they comply.

When I returned to movie theaters after the threat of COVID receded, I wondered if people would do any better at heeding the requests made before a screening to refrain from conversation and to silence their cell phones. I haven't noticed much improvement, and that makes me think that we resist silence because it requires that we listen to something other than the voice inside our heads. It asks us to pay close attention to what is before us, and many people are not willing to do that.

In recent years we have learned that places we once thought of as silent are not. We can now listen to the wild groans and shrieks of stars forming out of gases and dust in outer space. We hear the haunting songs of whales that allow them to communicate with other whales. People often complain about our noisy world, especially if they live in cities where the deep, steady thrum of freeway traffic is accompanied by car alarms, ambulance sirens, the loud bass of car stereos, and barking dogs. But we are likely to reject the silence required of us to watch a movie that lasts for two or three hours.

I worked for many years as a visiting poet in schools and devised an exercise for students. I would tell them that I wanted them to make as much noise as possible, provided that when I raised my hand, they'd stop immediately. The teachers looked aghast, but the students relished the chance to shout, stomp their feet, and pound on their desks. I tried (and usually succeeded) to stop the ruckus before a principal came by to investigate. Then I told the students that in the second part of this exercise, they were to create silence. No rolling of pencils on their desks, no fussing with the Velcro straps on their shoes, just sitting still enough to hear their breathing. I promised that the silence wouldn't last any longer than their noisy outburst. For the last part of the exercise, I asked them to write about what that silence had felt like.

Nature images prevailed: as silent as a tree, a blade of grass, the moon. But many students found that silence was scary. It unnerved them. One girl wrote that silence made her feel as if she was waiting for something, but she didn't know what it was. That sense of silence being expectant may be one major reason we distrust it. We prefer distraction to a silence that forces us back to our inmost selves and to the realization that the ultimate silence is death.

Monastic people are not afraid of either silence or waiting, and they tend to be realistic about their mortality. St. Benedict, in his rule of life for monks, instructs them to "day by day remind yourself that you are going to die."[1] Monks know that this is not a morbid preoccupation but a useful tool. When another person's behavior annoys them, remembering Benedict's admonition can curb the temptation to do or say something they will later regret. Anyone can try this: when you're stuck in a long, slow-moving line at the grocery store, or an inconsiderate driver cuts you off in traffic, remember that you and everyone around you will one day die. This changes your perspective and might give your irritation a chance to transform into tenderness, forgiveness, and even love. But it is not easy, and like many aspects of monastic life, it requires adjustment.

Into Great Silence, a documentary about the Carthusians, the most austere of the Christian monastic orders, eases us into a world we know little about and allows us to feel, when we depart, that the journey has been worthwhile. The film is a stunning immersion in monastic silence, perfectly capturing what it feels like to enter a monastery guest house: if you sit in your room for a while after you arrive, you can feel the silence sink into your bones. But I have never experienced the deafening silence that permeates a Carthusian house. Except when they gather every day to chant the Psalms in church, these monks are silent. They make the Benedictines look like playboys.

Carthusian monks live as hermits, praying regularly in their rooms and gathering daily for communal worship. Most meals are delivered through a hole in the door of their hermitages, but on Sundays and feast days the men have a silent meal together while a book is being read aloud. The monks also tend small gardens where they raise vegetables, fruits, and flowers.

Carthusians speak once a week, during a four-hour Sunday walk with other members of the community. We hear one such conversation in the film, and I was delighted to find the men gossiping good-naturedly about how other monasteries have abandoned some practices that these monks still use. Their everyday life is awash with signs and symbols, and one monk says, "When we abandon the signs, we tear down the walls of our house." Another adds, "We should look for their meaning and not question the signs but ourselves." Wisdom borne of silent reflection, looking deeply into oneself and resisting the temptation to choose easy answers.

Throughout the film we sense that the rhythms of these men's lives are in tune with the seasons. We watch icicles melt in spring and hear birdsong in summer. We enjoy the view of the spectacular mountain peaks and dense forests that surround the monastery. But the film also makes demands of us.

When I first saw it in a museum auditorium, about a third of the audience had left by the time it ended. Two-and-a-half hours of near silence was too much for many to take. And I must ask why. Are we so impatient to get on with our lives that we can't appreciate a movie in which "action" might consist of a man reading, kneeling in prayer, or chopping stalks of celery?

I can think of only one recent film, 2018's *A Quiet Place*, that contains less spoken dialogue than *Into Great Silence*, and it's a horror film. In a postapocalyptic world, blind monsters who have invaded the earth are intent on killing humans. One advertisement for the film reads, "If they hear you, they'll hunt you." Silence in *A Quiet Place* will help you survive, but it also feels like a punishment.

Many onlookers might feel that the silence of Carthusian life is punishing, but the monks find it liberating. The few spoken words in *Into Great Silence* come from an interview with a monk who has lived in silence for over sixty years. He asks, "Why be afraid of death? It's the fate of all humans." He feels that death means growing closer to God. "The closer one comes to God," he says, "the happier one is." He himself seems remarkably happy. We hear laughter when monks, on one of their weekly walks, take turns sliding and tumbling down a steep, snowy hill. The slapstick is welcome, and the men's merriment rings like a bell.

The making of this film is a story in itself. As the only guests Carthusians normally admit are men and women applying to join, their lives are mostly hidden. And that is fine with them. When in 1984 Philip Gröning first wrote to the abbot of the Grand Chartreuse, the original Carthusian monastery in the French Alps, seeking permission to make a documentary about the monks, the abbot replied that he'd get back to him. Sixteen years later he contacted Gröning and said that the community was ready.

What's sixteen years when you have eternity in mind? One reason Christian monastics have been around for seventeen hundred years is that they don't overvalue efficiency but allow things to happen in their own good time. Gröning and the monks agreed that he would shoot footage by himself, without a crew, and use only available light. Most significantly, there would be no voiceover narration, forcing viewers to embrace the film's imagery and interpret it for themselves.

Gröning has said that living in silence made him more aware of small things he might once have overlooked: a pile of white buttons for sewing onto habits, crocuses emerging in melting snow, packets of seeds for planting come spring, the beauty of sunlight on an old wooden floor. There is a scene of younger monks chopping wood; later we view an impressive floor-to-ceiling stacking of the firewood that will be the community's source of heat during the winter. We see the men caring for one another, giving haircuts or rubbing lotion onto the skin of a frail, elderly confrere. They work silently but offer each other engaging smiles. We glimpse a room near the entrance of the church where written notices are posted and mail is received.

This film shows us something that few people outside the Carthusian order have ever witnessed: the reception of two novices, in this case two young Black men, Etienne and Benjamin. We first see a monk measuring them so that he can sew their habits, and at the ceremony we witness an "embrace of peace" when each of the young men kneels before an older monk in turn. The elder must bow down to embrace the younger one. Gestures like these have great symbolic significance in the community: love made visible, without words.

The film also shows several "externs" who are not hermits but support the community in the barn, kitchen, and grounds. They don't wear the white habits of the hermits but habits of denim. We hear one extern speak tenderly to barn cats as he puts out bowls of food and water. We see another shoveling deep snow out of a row of garden beds. It's a strenuous job, but he does it patiently and well, giving the filmmaker a quick smile when he's done and can go into a shed to warm up.

Viewing options are always in flux, but as of this writing, *Into Great Silence* is available as a two-DVD set containing the film and several documentaries. As DVDs are rapidly becoming obsolete, I hope that all this material will soon be made available in other formats. One of the documentaries contains an insightful appreciation of the film by Cardinal Paul Poupard, who reminds us that the film asks us to enter a different space and time, which can provide a deep spiritual experience. In a fifty-three-minute night office, we see and hear the monks chant a service that begins a little after midnight each day. There is an extended interview with the elderly monk who insists that the past is a human concept and that we find God only in the present.

In one documentary, Gröning describes *Into Great Silence* as "a film for the ear," allowing the viewer to set aside the language that dominates our thinking and appreciate that "where words fail, sensations arise." As we hear the sounds of a monastery—footsteps, chanting, and bells—he also asks us to take a good look at "faces, buildings, landscapes, and work. Above all," Gröning writes, "there is time."[2] And that, I believe, is what frightens us about silence and about monks themselves. They embrace the reality of time passing in ways that most of us would rather ignore as we go about our lives.

Many of us daydream about simplifying our lives, ridding ourselves of unnecessary baggage, both physical and emotional, and enjoying a less busy and noisy life. Well, as I see it, the Carthusians are calling our bluff: if you really want to strip down to essentials, they can show you how. They've been doing it for nearly a thousand years.

Gareth

I first saw *Into Great Silence* in a theater forced to keep the lights half-up due to overly zealous health and safety regulations. Someone had insisted that the theater's exit signs weren't bright enough, so until such illumination could be installed, movies needed to be shown with such extreme ambient light that we could see other audience members even more clearly than the images on the screen. In one respect it made the experience of watching *Into Great Silence* impossible—the film invites such a depth of attention. But in another, it was a perfect viewing environment for a film about contemplation, for if part of the spiritual journey is to make peace with the uncontrollability of life, then I imagine the monks might offer a wry smile. If you can make appropriate peace with even a badly projected great film, then surely you're at least part of the way to wholeness.

If you accept its invitation, *Into Great Silence* does exactly what its title promises. It will draw you into a place and among people who may be more different from most you will ever visit or meet, but it will also serve as a mirror for the things your heart most wants.

Upon its original release, *Into Great Silence* packed out theaters in New York City for weeks, partly because people heard that there were places in Manhattan where three hours of contemplative quiet were available, several times a day, for the price of a movie ticket. Perhaps the museum audience with whom Kathleen saw the movie included too many people who were so used to the abundance of astonishment available (and quickly passed by) in many museums that they found it difficult to linger. The New York audiences may have included more people who staggered in from the thunderous streets knowing they couldn't afford *not* to give themselves over to such a generous serving of peace. Exchanging the cares of this world for the simplicity offered in this monastery, whether it costs sixteen dollars or your soul, doesn't seem like a bad deal at all.

As with all spiritual wisdom, the key is to allow the imagination to embrace universal truth in your particular life. Most of us are not called to monastic experience, at least not 24/7. But holy silences are not only available to us all but necessary if we are to uncover who we really are. The story that most captivates me says that humans are a little lower than the angels, bearers of the image of love, participants in love's further evolution, here to discover and embody life to the fullest, as individuals gifted to bring what we have to the table and in communities that invite us to ask for what we need. I don't know how you can get fully into that way of being without discovering silence at the heart of everything—God's first language, so they say. Whatever your conception of God, there is a great silence near the core of things.

This is not the same as emptiness. As Kathleen says, silence can be something you make. It must therefore *consist of something*. Is silence the sound between air and music? Is there a silence between the keystroke-clicking that helped form the shapes of the letters on this page? Is there a silence even *within* the drone of the refrigerator beside the table where I'm writing? It seems to me that those most versed in the experience of silence would suggest that while silence needs to be claimed, this is not because it is innately rare, just that we have constructed a world in which distortions of silence are more present than we should have allowed. But just as wise contemplatives throughout history have experienced the nearness of light in the darkest places, and comfort in the most distressing ones, silence is available even amid noise.

Even a movie theater that doesn't turn off the lights can be the location for a work of surpassing wonder to be seen at its best. That is, if we can tune into what is occurring beyond what the naked eye can perceive—*inside* the picture. On a building site the hum of equipment can be aligned with the frequency of *Om*, an airplane seat can be made a monk's cell, staying up late to write an essay about a movie can become an occasion for the writer to access the silence in his heart.

I know this to be true because *Into Great Silence*, nearly twenty years after that imperfectly perfect viewing, still speaks to me. The memory of the exquisite close-up images of these monks, Gröning's camera abiding much longer than we're used to—this memory is life-giving even now. It nudges me to imitate the gentle and slow move of the monk's head upward, looking across the room where there is no one looking back at me, yet I smile. I inhale, I smile again, and I say nothing, for these monks remind me of my wish to sink into a deeper, silent layer of the incarnation of love that my life, and yours, is intended to be.

As our first chapter explored, we each began our journey into embodiment by waiting. We did not know what we were waiting for, and the experience of birth was so shocking that it may have felt like dying. But as with the children Kathleen taught, the ruckus that attended our arrival gave way to the possibility of tranquility.

Permanent quiet is boring, just as much as perpetual noise is irritating. But tranquility is more easily treasured when its opposite is not erased, but welcome. (Thomas Merton went to jazz clubs even after he entered the monastery. Choosing silence does not have to mean choosing to be a curmudgeon.) And even those who have taken vows of silence will contend with interruptions—a plane overhead being just the most visible intrusion in the movie, and a reminder of the interruptions with which we must all make peace. Airplanes, or the news, or traffic, or busyness may jut in. But even if we could get rid of all human-made distractions, there would still be cicadas or ocean waves or the sound of our own breath. True silence hardly exists; indeed, people who have spent time in soundproof rooms say it nearly drove them mad. So we should not punish ourselves if we are distracted by a breezy air conditioner or a clanging door while trying silent meditation. The point of the great silence to which we're invited is not a complete absence of sound but a way of living beyond too much talk.

It makes sense to end this book with a movie about silence, which is also a movie about waiting. Waiting is where we will be invited to spend much of our lives. I love Kathleen's expression that if waiting seems impossible, instead of fretting about whatever it is we are waiting for, we can refuse to wait by giving ourselves to the presence of the present moment. If the silence we make in moments is part of the story of love, and if one of the reasons that monks have been around longer than the printing press, airplanes, or recorded music is that they don't value over-efficiency, perhaps our journey into a whole life through twelve movies could be well served by watching *Into Great Silence* again.

And again.

Questions and Conversations

1. When have you experienced silence without trying?
2. Have you ever chosen an experience of silence? What were the circumstances, and what did it lead to?

3. What do you know about the circumstances of your conception and the period between that and your birth?

4. What do you think of the idea that consciously claiming or making silence is a way of imitating the experience of our gestation in the womb, our first experience of waiting?

5. Does silence ever make you uneasy? Have you figured out why?

6. Could you live with as much silence and solitude as the monks in the film? Do you see any value in that?

7. Have you developed strategies for times when waiting is inevitable and promises to be frustrating and/or anxiety-inducing?

EPILOGUE

It's Still a Beautiful Day

Gareth

If it weren't for cinema . . .

I might not have felt seen as a lonely kid wanting to do something meaningful with my life (*E.T.*, *The Goonies*, and *The Red Balloon*).

I might not have thought about how the distance between people grows when we fear telling the truth or asking for help (*Crimes and Misdemeanors*, *Jean de Florette*, *Fanny and Alexander*, *Make Way for Tomorrow*).

I might not know that impudence can also telegraph creativity (*Lawrence of Arabia*).

I would not have memories of spectacular, delicate, often exquisite imagery of the natural and built landscape and how we steward or disregard it (*Koyaanisqatsi*, *Baraka*, *Wall-E*, *The Abyss*).

My internal conversation would not be funded by cautionary tales of egotistical ambition or humility before being

(*Citizen Kane*, *The Life and Death of Colonel Blimp*, *Andrei Rublev*, *2001: A Space Odyssey*, *Ikiru*), challenging invocations to follow an inner compass no matter the cost (*On the Waterfront*, *The Assassin*, *Malcolm X*, *8½*), revelatory dreams about the meaning of death (*After Life*), and explorations of power and justice (*Do the Right Thing*, *Hiroshima Mon Amour*, *Cabaret*). Or a motley crew or couple of stumblers looking for answers and finding community (*The Muppet Movie*, *The Royal Tenenbaums*, *The Apartment*), or broken people staying broken because the social contract is broken too (*Midnight Cowboy*) or overcoming their brokenness by making a new social contract (*Lone Star*). I would not have in the back of my mind the illustration of spending a life on love with which *The Exorcist* culminates; or the empathy induced by *One Flew over the Cuckoo's Nest*, *Wings of Desire*, and *Where Is the Friend's House?*; or the confrontation with desperation revealed in *Thelma & Louise*, *Revanche*, *The Piano*, and *The Dam Keeper*.

I might not have the comfort of imaginary friends reminding me that my questions, confusions, and griefs are welcome (*The Apartment*, *The Fisher King*, *The Accidental Tourist*, *All About My Mother*).

I would not have gone to India, Japan, Brazil, Mexico, China, Argentina, Romania, Egypt, and Italy, all without leaving my living room.

I wouldn't have been awakened by off-the-beaten-track movies, my love for which makes me feel like I'm part of a small but noble band: *Endless Poetry*, *Wonderstruck*, *Patti Cakes*, *The Painter and the Thief*, *Le Havre*, *Ratcatcher*, *The Barbarian Invasions*, *Ten Canoes*, *Russian Ark*, *Kundun*, *The Hudsucker Proxy*, *Basquiat*, *Smoke*, *The Addiction*, *Nelly et Monsieur Arnaud*, *Grace of My Heart*, *To Sleep with Anger*, *Mississippi Masala*, and a hundred more besides.

And I might not have experienced the elevation that helps convince me that there's more to life than what we can describe or see, as in *Fearless, The New World, Embrace of the Serpent, A.I. Artificial Intelligence, Yi-Yi, In the Mood for Love, The Fountain, Atanarjuat: The Fast Runner*, and *Moonlight*.

My doubts and loves would not have a cinematic soundtrack or backdrop. My life is unthinkable without the movies, and for years now they've been the ongoing conversation that I share with my coauthor and friend. The next time I see a movie, I'll open my mind and heart, and with gratitude let my own dreams mingle with those projected in front of me. That gratitude mingles today with what I feel for you, the readers of this book. May your experience of cinema help you experience more of the wholeness of your life. Thank you.

Kathleen

I have been reading since I was four years old, but movies were not a part of my life until I was about eight. In the 1950s, parents often included a theater outing in birthday parties, which meant that I saw my first films, *Old Yeller* and *The Shaggy Dog*, distracted by kids who were more interested in throwing popcorn at each other than watching the movie.

I began to take films seriously when I was in my teens and was blessed, when I was in my early twenties, to be living in New York City at a time when so many theaters were showing classics and foreign films. It was then that I embarked on my haphazard education in cinema.

The late Senegalese filmmaker Ousmane Sembène, a fisherman's son, beat the odds in a highly stratified society, taught himself to read and write in French, and published several novels in the 1950s. At the time, well over 80 percent of Senegalese were illiterate, and Sembène realized that if he wanted to reach most of his countrymen, he had to turn to film. He called movies "the night school of the people."[1]

Even though literacy rates around the world have improved in the last hundred years, Sembène's phrase has stayed with me, reminding me of one reason films matter. They can reach people in a way that books cannot. In these concluding remarks I hope to reflect on some of the recommended films in the list Gareth and I have provided, films that have illuminated and informed my life.

The Quiet Girl, An Education, and *The Souvenir* hit uncomfortably close to home. I was the kind of "quiet girl" who kept emotions bottled up inside, and these films helped me understand that this made me vulnerable as a young woman to seduction by older men and slow to recognize that the romance they offered was a trap.

Endless Poetry, the autobiographical masterpiece by Alejandro Jodorowsky, has a particular relevance for me. When Jodorowsky's *El Topo,* a surrealistic and acidly comic spoof of Westerns, began the first-ever midnight showings at a Manhattan "art house" theater, I was one of the young people who was drawn to it. Many scenes made me laugh, but I also found the film self-indulgent. I later met Jodorowsky at a party—he was twenty years my senior and struck me as vain and egotistical. But years later when I encountered his *Endless Poetry,* a film he made at the age of eighty-eight, it reminded me that people change in remarkable ways. I am no longer a young woman harboring a false sense of my own sophistication, and while Jodorowsky will always be a wild man, confrontational, zany, and self-absorbed, he is also capable of making an engaging, thoughtful, and moving film about the life of an artist.

The little movie theater on Main Street in Lemmon, South Dakota, still has wall sconces that date from the 1920s when my mother watched *Flash Gordon* serials there as a child. The community treasures the theater so much that it raised funds so that it could switch to a digital format instead of closing. First-run Hollywood films now show there on weekends. As rural people are generally ignored in the American media, I'm grateful that two films—*The Last Picture Show* and *Nebraska*—do an excellent job of depicting people I know. *The Last Picture Show* explores the currents that run deep beneath the surface in any small town. Many young people are desperate to leave; others cannot imagine moving away. There are personal tragedies that a facade of social niceties doesn't quite conceal. *Nebraska* makes me feel as if I'm visiting relatives in Iowa and the Dakotas. I have been on that forlorn-looking Main Street and staggered through conversations about the weather with folks who are champion slow-talkers. The film made me wish my parents were still alive because they would love it.

Cries and Whispers is the first film that caused me to confront the subject of grave illness and death, and how different family members respond to it, and the many ways they grieve. I return to it often because now that I have tended to members of my family as they were dying, the film continues to provide new revelations and new meaning.

Like Gareth, I have been invigorated by the way films open the world for me. Lee Isaac Chung, in his autobiographical film *Minari*, explores the interior world of a family whose circumstances are far different from my own.

The film depicts a boy whose father, a Korean immigrant, is determined to be a farmer and, despite his wife's wariness, purchases land in Arkansas on which he plans to grow vegetables to sell to a growing Korean population. The heart of the film is not on large themes like immigration but on the dynamics of family life, the couple's squabbles and concerns over making enough to live on, and the upheaval caused when the wife's newly widowed mother comes from Korea and must share a room with her grandson. *Minari* caused me to reflect on the conflicts in my own family but also on the love that continues to hold us together, despite our many differences.

Circumstances led Chung to live in Rwanda for a time, and he made his first film, *Munyurangabo*, there, employing local people, all nonprofessional actors. It's the first movie ever made in the Rwandan dialect of Kinyarwanda. But those details matter less than the substance that concerns Chung, the horrific Rwandan genocide of 1994. The film's two main characters are teenage boys who are too young to have experienced it. One is a Hutu and one a Tutsi, and they are attempting to resist the warnings of their elders that their differing tribal heritage means that they should not associate with each other. Their friendship is complicated by the desire of one boy to take revenge on the man who killed his father.

Chung demonstrates that it is possible to tell a complex story in a simple way and to produce a parable about the aftermath of brutal violence and the forgiveness that is possible for ordinary people to attain. That to me is the essence of what I most admire in the art of cinema. Chung takes me to an unfamiliar place, and I meet people there who share my concerns about how to live honorably in a cruel and unjust world.

I hope that you will enjoy watching and discussing the films we've featured in this book, and I thank you for taking this journey with us.

FOR FURTHER VIEWING

Chapter 1: Waiting to Be Born

Andrei Rublev (USSR, 1966, directed by Andrei Tarkovsky, written by Andrei Tarkovsky and Andrei Konchalovsky)

Birth Story: Ina May Gaskin and the Farm Midwives (USA, 2012, directed by Mary Wigmore and Sarah Lamb)

Children of Men (UK/USA/Japan, 2006, directed by Alfonso Cuarón, written by Alfonso Cuarón, David Arata, Mark Fergus, and Hawk Ostby)

Interstellar (USA, 2014, directed by Christopher Nolan, written by Christopher Nolan and Jonathan Nolan)

The Road (USA, 2009, directed by John Hillcoat, written by Joe Penhall, from the novel by Cormac McCarthy)

Solaris (USSR, 1972, directed by Andrei Tarkovsky, written by Andrei Tarkovsky and Friedrich Gorenstein, from the novel by Stanisław Lem)

Chapter 2: Childhood

The Dam Keeper (USA, 2014, directed and written by Robert Kondo and Daisuke Tsutsumi)

Fanny and Alexander (Sweden, 1982, directed and written by Ingmar Bergman)

Marriage Story (USA, 2019, directed and written by Noah Baumbach)

Minari (USA, 2020, directed and written by Lee Isaac Chung)

Queen of Katwe (USA, 2016, directed by Mira Nair, written by William Wheeler, based on the book by Tim Crothers)

The Quiet Girl (Ireland, 2022, directed and written by Colm Bairéad, from the novella by Claire Keegan)

The Red Balloon (France, 1956, directed and written by Albert Lamorisse)

Whale Rider (Aotearoa/New Zealand, 2002, directed and written by Niki Caro, based on the book by Witi Ihimaera)

Where Is the Friend's House? (Iran, 1987, directed and written by Abbas Kiarostami)

Wonderstruck (USA, 2017, directed by Todd Haynes, written by Brian Selznick)

Chapter 3: Community

The Antidote (USA, 2020, directed by Kahane Cooperman and John Hoffman)

The Circle (Iran, 2000, directed by Jafar Panahi, written by Kambuzia Partovi and Jafar Panahi)

Lars and the Real Girl (USA, 2007, directed by Craig Gillespie, written by Nancy Oliver)

The Last Picture Show (USA, 1971, directed by Peter
Bogdanovich, written by Peter Bogdanovich and
Larry McMurtry)

Powwow Highway (USA, 1989, directed by Jonathan
Wacks, written by David Seals, Janet Heaney, and
Jean Stawarz, from the novel by Seals)

Skins (USA, 2002, directed by Chris Eyre, written by
Adrian C. Louis and Jennifer D. Lyne, from the novel
by Adrian C. Louis)

Smoke (USA, 1995, directed and written by Wayne
Wang and Paul Auster)

Tillsammans (Sweden, 2000, directed and written by
Lukas Moodysson)

Chapter 4: The Breaking and Remaking of Self

Casablanca (USA, 1942, directed by Michael Curtiz,
written by Julius J. Epstein, Philip G. Epstein, and
Howard Koch)

Endless Poetry (France/Chile, 2015, directed and written
by Alejandro Jodorowsky)

Ikiru (Japan, 1952, directed by Akira Kurosawa, written
by Akira Kurosawa, Shinobu Hashimoto, and Hideo
Nguni)

Living (UK, 2023, directed by Oliver Hermanus, screenplay by Kazuo Ishiguro)

Mass Appeal (USA, 1984, directed by Glenn Jordan,
written by Bill C. Davis)

On the Waterfront (USA, 1954, directed by Elia Kazan,
written by Elia Kazan, Budd Schulberg, and Malcolm
Johnson)

Stranger Than Fiction (USA, 2006, directed by Marc
Forster, written by Zach Helm)

True Confessions (USA, 1981, directed by Ulu Grosbard, written by John Gregory Dunne, Joan Didion, and Gary S. Hall)

Chapter 5: Vocation—Meaning in the Ordinary

Bend It Like Beckham (UK/USA/Germany, 2002, directed by Gurinder Chadha, written by Gurinder Chadha, Paul Mayeda Berges, and Guljit Bindra)

Crouching Tiger, Hidden Dragon (China/Taiwan/Hong Kong/USA, 2000, directed by Ang Lee, written by Wang Hui-ling, James Schamus, and Tsai Kuo-jung, based on the novel by Wang Dulu)

Daughters of the Dust (USA, 1991, directed and written by Julie Dash)

An Education (UK/USA, 2009, directed by Lone Scherfig, written by Nick Hornby, based on the memoir by Lynn Barber)

Ida (Poland/France/Denmark/UK, 2013, directed by Paweł Pawlikowski, written by Paweł Pawlikowski and Rebecca Lenkiewicz)

Little Women (USA, 2019, directed and written by Greta Gerwig, based on the novel by Louisa May Alcott)

Nebraska (USA, 2013, directed by Alexander Payne, written by Bob Nelson)

Samsara (India/Germany/France/Italy/Switzerland, 2001, directed by Pan Nalin, written by Pan Nalin and Tim Baker)

See You Yesterday (USA, 2019, directed by Stefon Bristol, written by Stefon Bristol and Fredrica Bailey, based on their short film)

Silence (USA/Taiwan/Mexico/UK, 2016, directed by
  Martin Scorsese, written by Martin Scorsese and Jay
  Cocks, from the novel by Shūsaku Endō)
The Souvenir (UK/USA, 2019, directed and written by
  Joanna Hogg)

Chapter 6: Vocation—To Step into Your Own Shoes

First Man (USA, 2018, directed by Damien Chazelle,
  written by Josh Singer)
Gandhi (USA/UK/India, 1982, directed by Richard
  Attenborough, written by John Bailey)
Harriet (USA, 2019, directed by Kasi Lemmons, written
  by Kasi Lemmons and Gregory Allen Howard)
A Hidden Life (Austria/Germany/Italy/USA, 2019, di-
  rected and written by Terrence Malick)
Selma (USA, 2014, directed by Ava DuVernay, written
  by Paul Webb)
Taxi (Iran, 2015, directed and written by Jafar Panahi)
There Is No Evil (Iran, 2020, directed and written by
  Mohammad Rasoulof)

Chapter 7: Relationships

The Before Trilogy (USA, 1995–2013, directed by Richard Linklater, written by Richard Linklater, Kim Kri-
  zan, Ethan Hawke, and Julie Delpy)
Close (Belgium, 2022, directed by Lukas Dhont, written
  by Lukas Dhont and Angelo Tijssens)
Eternal Sunshine of the Spotless Mind (USA, 2004,
  directed by Michel Gondry, written by Charlie
  Kaufman)

I Was a Simple Man (USA, 2021, directed and written by Christopher Makoto Yogi)

Midnight Cowboy (USA, 1969, directed by John Schlesinger, written by Waldo Salt, from the novel by James Leo Herlihy)

Supernova (UK, 2020, directed and written by Harry Macqueen)

Thelma & Louise (USA, 1991, directed by Ridley Scott, written by Callie Khouri)

Chapter 8: Overcoming Success

The Duellists (UK, 1977, directed by Ridley Scott, written by Gerald Vaughan-Hughes)

A Face in the Crowd (USA, 1957, directed by Elia Kazan, written by Budd Schulberg)

Fearless (USA, 1993, directed by Peter Weir, written by Rafael Yglesias)

The Piano (Aotearoa/New Zealand, 1993, directed and written by Jane Campion)

Stories We Tell (Canada, 2012, directed and written by Sarah Polley)

Sweet Smell of Success (USA, 1957, directed by Alexander Mackendrick, written by Clifford Odets)

The Verdict (USA, 1982, directed by Sidney Lumet, written by David Mamet)

Chapter 9: Generosity

Life Is Beautiful (Italy, 1997, directed and written by Roberto Benigni)

A *Matter of Life and Death* (UK, 1946, directed and written by Michael Powell and Emeric Pressburger)

Where Is the Friend's House? (Iran, 1987, directed and written by Abbas Kiarostami)

Chapter 10: Transforming Conflict

The Abyss (USA, 1989, directed and written by James Cameron)

As It Is in Heaven (Sweden, 2004, directed by Kay Pollak, written by Kay Pollak, Anders Nyberg, Ola Olsson, Carin Pollak, and Margaretha Pollak)

Bulletproof Heart (USA, 1994, directed by Mark Malone, written by Gordon Melbourne)

Mass (USA, 2021, directed and written by Fran Kranz)

Munich (USA, 2005, directed by Steven Spielberg, written by Tony Kushner)

Munyurangabo (Rwanda/USA, 2007, directed by Lee Isaac Chung, written by Lee Isaac Chung and Samuel Gray Anderson)

Past Lives (USA, 2023, directed and written by Celine Song)

Secrets & Lies (UK, 1996, directed and written by Mike Leigh)

Wolfwalkers (Ireland/Luxembourg/France, 2020, directed by Tomm Moore and Ross Stewart, written by Will Collins)

Chapter 11: Death and Beyond

Cries and Whispers (Sweden, 1972, directed and written by Ingmar Bergman)

Departures (Japan, 2008, directed by Yojiro Takita,
   written by Kundo Koyama)
Field of Dreams (USA, 1989, directed and written by
   Phil Alden Robinson, based on the novel *Shoeless Joe*
   by W. P. Kinsella)
Marina Abramović: The Artist Is Present (USA, 2012,
   directed by Matthew Akers and Jeff Dupre)
Ordinary Love (UK/Ireland, 2019, directed by Lisa
   Barros D'Sa and Glenn Leyburn, written by Owen
   McCafferty)
The Seventh Seal (Sweden, 1957, directed and written
   by Ingmar Bergman, based on his play *Trämålning*)
Soul (USA, 2020, directed by Pete Docter, written by
   Pete Docter, Mike Jones, and Kemp Powers)
Wristcutters: A Love Story (UK/USA, 2006, directed and
   written by Goran Dukić)

Chapter 12: Waiting in Silence

In Pursuit of Silence (USA, 2015, directed by Patrick
   Shen)
The Tree of Life (USA, 2011, directed and written by
   Terrence Malick)
Wall-E (USA, 2008, directed by Andrew Stanton, writ-
   ten by Andrew Stanton and Jim Reardon)

ACKNOWLEDGMENTS

Gareth: I'd like to acknowledge everyone who has ever watched and discussed a movie with me, especially Greg Feightner and Tamara Hanna Feightner; Alexander Field, who got the book to Brazos, who have taken good care of it; Katelyn Beaty, the chief giver of said care; Barry Taylor, who makes me laugh and makes me think; and most of all Brian Ammons, who is always my first reader and whose wisdom about vocation and filmmaking as a collaborative art and an experience shared with the audience mirrors the way the book has been written.

Kathleen: I also owe a debt of gratitude to Alexander Field and Katelyn Beaty and the staff at Brazos. And I would like to acknowledge the many people who have helped shape my spirituality and my love of cinema. They are too many to name, but they know who they are. And as always, I want to thank my family for all the support and encouragement they have given me, especially David and Rebecca, my best movie partners. I miss you.

NOTES

Introduction

1. Mira Nair, interview by Gareth Higgins, "A Conversation with Mira Nair," *Image*, issue 93, https://imagejournal.org/article/conversation -mira-nair.
2. Stephen Sundborg, quoted in Thomas N. Hart, *Spiritual Quest: A Guide to the Changing Landscape* (New York: Paulist Press, 1999), 40.

Chapter 1 Waiting to Be Born

1. *The Dialogue of Catherine of Siena*, trans. Suzanne Noffke (New York: Paulist Press, 1980).
2. Lawrence M. Krauss, *Quantum Man: Richard Feynman's Life in Science* (New York: Norton, 2011).

Chapter 2 Childhood

1. Henry James, *What Maisie Knew* (1897), introduction, available at https://www.gutenberg.org/files/7118/7118-h/7118-h.htm.
2. Alice Hutchison, "The Value of Poetry in Political Conflict: An Imagine Festival Conversation with Michael Longley," March 25, 2022, Shared Future News, https://sharedfuture.news/the-value-of-poetry-in -political-conflict-an-imagine-festival-conversation-with-michael-longley.
3. Alan Watts, "The Nature of Consciousness," lecture, 1969, available at https://www.organism.earth/library/document/out-of-your-mind-2.

Chapter 3 Community

This chapter discusses two movies that we consider to be companion pieces that fit very well together. Stories that have been told only at the fringes of "mainstream" culture—in this case, stories of Native American people—are thankfully finding a more central place.

1. I spell northern Ireland with a lowercase *n* as a way of encouraging dialogue about transforming the divided community relationships in the place where I'm from.

Chapter 6 Vocation—To Step into Your Own Shoes

1. Peniel E. Joseph, "Why We Have to Reckon with the Real Malcolm X," *New York Times*, November 18, 2023, https://www.nytimes.com/2023/11/18/opinion/malcolm-x-legacy-opera.html.

2. Charles Eisenstein, "What Is It Like to Be You?," CharlesEisenstein.org, accessed March 1, 2024, https://charleseisenstein.org/videos/video/what-is-it-like-to-be-you.

3. Delroy Lindo, interview, special features in *Malcolm X*, directed by Spike Lee (1992; New York: Criterion Collection, 2022), Blu-ray.

4. Barry Michael Cooper, interview, special features in *Malcolm X*, directed by Spike Lee (1992; New York: Criterion Collection, 2022), Blu-ray.

5. *The Psalms: An Inclusive Language Version Based on the Grail Translation from the Hebrew* (Chicago: GIA Publications, 1986), s.v. "Psalm 137."

6. *Psalms*, s.v. "Psalm 137."

7. Malcolm X, *The Autobiography of Malcolm X* (1965; repr., New York: Random House, 2015), 421.

8. Malcolm X, *Autobiography of Malcolm X*, 416.

9. Malcolm X, *Autobiography of Malcolm X*, 439.

10. Roger Ebert, "Malcolm X," RogerEbert.com, November 18, 1992, https://www.rogerebert.com/reviews/malcolm-x-1992.

Chapter 7 Relationships

This chapter discusses two movies that we feel fit very well together and tell stories about people who have often been relegated to the margins, misrepresented, or worse. Here we're exploring stories about elderly people and members of the LGBTQ+ community.

1. Orson Welles, cited in "Peter Bogdanovich on *Make Way for Tomorrow*," Criterion Collection (website), May 18, 2015, https://www.criterion.com/current/posts/3560-peter-bogdanovich-on-make-way-for-tomorrow.

2. "First Differentiation-Based Approach to Marital and Sexual Therapy," Crucible Institute, https://crucible4points.com/about-crucible-therapy.

Chapter 8 Overcoming Success

1. Owen Myers, "Agnès Varda's Last Interview: 'I Fought for Radical Cinema All My Life,'" *Guardian*, March 29, 2019, https://www.theguardian

.com/film/2019/mar/29/agnes-varda-last-interview-i-fought-for-radical
-cinema-all-my-life.

2. Myers, "Agnès Varda's Last Interview."

3. A. O. Scott, "'Varda by Agnès' Review: A Final Visit with an Irreplaceable Filmmaker," *New York Times*, November 21, 2019, https://www.nytimes.com/2019/11/21/movies/varda-by-agnes-review.html.

Chapter 9 Generosity

1. *Letters I*, vol. 48 of *Luther's Works*, American Edition, ed. and trans. Gottfried G. Krodel (Philadelphia: Fortress, 1963), 281–82.

2. adrienne maree brown, "Excerpt from Sublevel: Report," adrienne mareebrown.net, March 12, 2018, https://adriennemareebrown.net/2018/03/12/excerpt-from-sublevel-report.

3. *The Psalms: An Inclusive Language Version Based on the Grail Translation from the Hebrew* (Chicago: GIA Publications, 1986), 122–23.

4. *Psalms*, 122–23.

Chapter 10 Transforming Conflict

1. Richard Rohr, *Things Hidden: Scripture as Spirituality* (Cincinnati: Franciscan Media, 2022).

Chapter 12 Waiting in Silence

1. Rule of St. Benedict, chapter 4, "The Tools for Good Works," verse 47.

2. Special features in *Into Great Silence*, directed by Philip Gröning (New York: Zeitgeist Films, 2005), DVD. See also the article "Voyage into Silence: Interview with Philip Gröning," Decent Films, accessed April 10, 2024, https://decentfilms.com/articles/groning.

Epilogue

1. *Sembène: The Making of African Cinema*, directed by Manthia Diawara and Ngugi Wa Thiong'o (1994; New York: Criterion Collection, 2008), DVD.

Kathleen Norris is an award-winning poet and the author of five *New York Times* bestsellers, including *The Cloister Walk* and *Dakota: A Spiritual Geography*. She writes frequently for *Give Us This Day*, a monthly publication from Liturgical Press. She speaks regularly at colleges, churches, and teaching hospitals, and is on the board of the St. John's School of Theology and Seminary in Collegeville, Minnesota.

Gareth Higgins is an Irish writer and storyteller. He is the cofounder of spirituality and creativity festivals, including Wild Goose, The Porch Gathering, and Movies and Meaning. He shares the leadership of *The Porch* community and is the author of *How Not to Be Afraid* and coauthor of *The Seventh Story*. He has been involved in peacebuilding and violence reduction and leads transformative story retreats in northern Ireland and the US.

Connect with Kathleen

Facebook: Kathleen Norris

Instagram @knorriseyt

Connect with Gareth

www.garethhiggins.net

www.theporchcommunity.net

Facebook Gareth Higgins

Instagram @garethihiggins

Kathleen and Gareth cowrite the weekly Soul Telegram newsletter on movies and meaning at www.soultelegram.com.